The Life and Times of
GEORGE V

OVERLEAF LEFT The Royal Family at
Buckingham Palace in 1913, painted by
Sir John Lavery. With King George and
Queen Mary are the Prince of Wales,
later Edward VIII, and the Princess Royal.
RIGHT Three medals from the war years
known to soldiers as 'Pip, Squeak and
Wilfred'. From left to right, the 1914 Star,
the British War Medal, the
Victory Medal.

The Life and Times of
GEORGE V

Denis Judd

Introduction by Antonia Fraser

Weidenfeld and Nicolson
London

Acknowledgments
page 6

1
Queen Victoria's
Grandson
1865–82
page 13

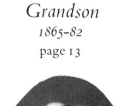

To my parents,
who knew George v's reign,
and to my wife, who did not

5
King
and Country
1914–18
page 122

© George Weidenfeld and Nicolson Limited
and Book Club Associates 1973

Reprinted and reissued 1993

All rights reserved. No part of this publication may be reproduced, stored in a retrieval system, or transmitted, in any form or by any means, electronic, mechanical, photocopying, recording or otherwise, without the prior written permission of the copyright owner.

Series designed by Paul Watkins
Layout by Sheila Sherwen

Filmset by Keyspools Limited, Golborne, Lancs
Printed and bound in Great Britain by
Butler & Tanner Ltd, Frome and London

Contents

Introduction
page 7

Author's Preface
page 9

2
Sailor Prince and Heir Presumptive
1882–1901
page 36

3
Prince of Wales
1901–10
page 64

4
King Amid Crisis
1910–14
page 92

6
A Fit Land for Heroes
1918–24
page 152

7
Storms, Calms and Uncertain Courses
1924–31
page 174

8
Towards the Jubilee
1931–6
page 198

Genealogical tree
page 218

Select bibliography
page 220

Index
page 222

Acknowledgments

Photographs and illustrations are supplied by, or reproduced by kind permission of the following. The pictures on pages 34, 39, 48–9, 52/2, *93*, *114-5*, 189, 213 are reproduced by gracious permission of HM the Queen; Bassano and Vandyk Studios: 11; Conway Picture Library: 52/3, 62-3, 67, 107, 105/2, 156, 164, 166/1, 166/2, 167/1, 167/2, 196-7, 210; Mary Evans Picture Library: 65; Major Gerald Flint-Shipman: *195*; John Freeman: 55; Guildhall Library and Art Gallery: 69, 70-1, 87, 88, 138, *206-7*; Imperial War Museum: 124, *126/1*, *126/2*, *126/3*, *126-7*, *127*, 130, 133, 134, 137, 141, 146-7; India Office Library: 105/1; A.F.Kersting: *14*; London Museum: *96/1*, *96/2*; Mansell Collection: 17, 20, 31, 43, 57, 58-9, 83, 112, 117; National Maritime Museum: *84/1*, *84/2*; National Monuments Record: 184; National Portrait Gallery: *15*, 187, *194*; Paul Popper: *15*, 53, 60, 94, 119, 142-3, 208/1, 211, 214/1, 214/2, 215; Press Association: 102, 116, 157/1, 157/2; Punch: 86, 176; Radio Times Hulton Picture Library: 10, 12, 18, 19, 23, 26, 27, 29, 30, 37, 50, 52/1, 66, 82, 90-1, 99, 108, 110, 111, 120-1, 123, 128, 139, 150-1, 153, 161, 170, 172-3, 175, 181, 182, 190-1, 199/1, 199/2, 202-3, 208/2, 209, 216; Roger-Viollet: 77; Derek Witty: *81*.

Picture research by Andra Nelki.

Numbers in italics refer to colour illustrations.

Introduction

WHAT A CONTRAST exists between the orderly popular image of King George V and the tumultuous course of his twenty-five year rule over Britain and her then still far flung Empire! On the one hand we have the bearded ex-naval officer, the stern but kindly *paterfamilias*, born in the Victorian age and retaining many of its attitudes. On the other, there are the events of the reign itself, whose very names recall a series of violent clashes – the early Ulster crisis, which had the effect of distracting the King's ministers from the imminent outbreak of the First World War, that blood-stained struggle itself, then return to the whole unremitting Irish question, and all this is to ignore domestic dramas which included the 1909–11 House of Lords furore, the successful demands of the suffragettes, the rise of the British Labour Party, the General Strike of 1926, and the further crisis which lead to a National Government under Ramsay MacDonald in 1931.

Prince George Frederick, born in 1865, the younger son of the future King Edward VII, might seem at first sight ill-equipped to preside over such a complex and changing period. Lacking the glamour of his beautiful mother Alexandra or the rumbustuous personality of his father, he was surely ideally suited for the naval career for which, as second son, he was initially trained. Yet the death of his elder brother in 1892 brought young George with 'his bright merry face' as his mother lovingly described it, into the direct line of the throne. It was a prominence further emphasised by his prompt marriage to the girl who had been his brother's destined bride, the admirable if reserved Princess May of Teck, who as our own Queen Mary was to carve her own niche in British history and legend.

How was such an essentially ordinary, upright man to cope with the many problems which flocked upon the monarchy unremittingly from George V's accession in 1910 until his death in 1936? In this new biography, Denis Judd's answer is both unexpected and fascinating. To a remarkable extent, King George v was in fact the right man in the right place, or at any rate occupying it at the right time. 'The naval demands of discipline and common-sense, the tolerance and good fellowship required in the mess-room' as the author puts it, turned out to be an appropriate training for a man who reigned at the moment when the British Empire reached its territorial zenith. Most importantly, George v proved above all his worth as a constitutional monarch and as Denis Judd so ably points out, that is the role by which he should most fairly be judged – one in which he was certainly head and shoulders above his predecessors. It was in answer to H.G. Wells' critical republican references to 'an alien and uninspiring court' that the King replied robustly: 'I may be uninspiring but I'm damned if I'm an alien.' In his usual straightforward way, he spoke the truth. Not only did he enjoy 'an enviable *rapport*' with his people, rooted in their deepest feelings of respect; it was also symbolic that George v should have deliberately founded the new House of Windsor in 1917. For his inspiration consisted in setting the pace for a constitutional monarchy, the possession of which still makes Britain the envy of the world.

Antonia Fraser

Author's preface

ANY AUTHOR who attempts to write 'The Life and Times of George V' must readily acknowledge his debt to Sir Harold Nicolson's masterly official biography. There are two main areas of indebtedness: one is to the impeccable quality of the writing, the other is to the copious quotations from George V's diary and letters, sources which are not available to the 'unofficial' biographer. Not that this book sets out to be a full biography, either official or unofficial; rather it seeks to place King George's life within its late nineteenth- and early twentieth-century contexts. Given the tumultuous and complex character of these years, and the considerable amount of recent historical analysis, this is a challenging task in itself, but one that has been lightened by the help and encouragement of my publishers – especially John Curtis and Celia Clear.

DENIS JUDD
London, 1973

1 Queen Victoria's

Grandson 1865-82

WHEN PRINCE GEORGE was born at 1.30 a.m. on 3 June 1865, it was barely two months since General Lee had surrendered the Army of Northern Virginia to General Grant at Appomattox, thus bringing the American Civil War effectively to an end. In Britain, William Ewart Gladstone was Chancellor of the Exchequer, and Dr Livingstone was about to publish his *Narrative of an Expedition to the Zambesi and Its Tributaries*. In the same year Mrs Gaskell died, and so did Lord Palmerston, independent to the last and preferring the Belgian Treaty to the Bible as death-bed reading.

Less weighty, though within a limited circle no less significant, matters attended the birth of the baby prince. He was the second son of Edward, Prince of Wales, and Princess Alexandra of Denmark, and he had to be named. His grandmother Queen Victoria, a widow in deepest mourning for nearly four years past, had strong views on family names. The Prince of Wales wrote to his formidable mother informing her that he and Princess Alexandra wished to christen the baby George Frederick. Queen Victoria replied:

> I fear I cannot admire the names you propose to give the Baby. I had hoped for some fine old name. Frederick is, however, the best of the two, and I hope you will *call* him so. *George* only came in with the Hanoverian family.
>
> However, if the dear child grows up good and wise, I shall not mind what his name is. Of course you will add *Albert* at the end, like your brothers, as you know we settled *long ago* that *all* dearest Papa's *male* descendants should bear *that* name, to mark *our line*, just as I wish all the girls to have Victoria after theirs.
>
> I lay great stress on this; and it is done in a great many families!

The Prince of Wales, who failed to see eye to eye with his mother on a wide variety of issues both great and small, replied, 'We are sorry to hear that you don't like the names we propose to give our little boy, but they are names that we like and have decided on for some time.' However, before the baby prince was christened at St George's Chapel, Windsor, on 7 July, a family compromise had taken place and he was named George Frederick Ernest Albert. His family were invariably to call him Georgie.

Prince George Frederick took his place in a royal family which was by no means free from public and private criticism.

PREVIOUS PAGES Prince George and his grandmother, Queen Victoria.

OPPOSITE Alexandra, Princess of Wales, holding the baby Prince George who was born in Marlborough House in 1865.

ABOVE Sandringham House in Norfolk was the favourite home of Edward and Alexandra. Prince George was deeply attached to the estate and described it as 'the place I love better than anywhere in the world.'
OPPOSITE
Princess Alexandra by Sir Luke Fildes.

Queen Victoria's grief for her dead husband had plunged her into a mourning seclusion that was causing adverse comment. A constitutional monarchy was all very well, but when the monarch was draped in black, shrouded from public view and apparently reluctant to attend to the duties of state, then maybe the system should be changed? Republican sentiment was certainly encouraged by the Queen's withdrawal, and the Prince of Wales told his mother in February 1869, 'We live in radical times, and the more the *People see the Sovereign* the better it is for the *People* and the *Country*.' It was the general relief at

the Prince of Wales's successful fight against typhoid in 1871, however, which dealt republicanism its most crushing blow, rather than Queen Victoria's gradual emergence from seclusion.

Nobody, however, could accuse the Prince of Wales of solitary tastes. He could hardly ever bear to be left alone, and his activities were essentially gregarious – gambling, horse-racing and party-going. He also pursued a variety of women with ardour. A good many of them failed to resist their royal suitor. While such affairs were conducted with discretion, the Prince of Wales's public reputation escaped censorious comment. But in 1870 he was called as witness in the Mordaunt divorce case. Sir Charles Mordaunt filed a petition for divorce from his young wife, citing two of the Prince's friends as co-respondents. When he appeared in the witness box, the Prince denied that he had committed adultery with Lady Mordaunt and was not cross-examined on the point.

For several weeks after the Mordaunt divorce proceedings, the Prince and Princess of Wales were occasionally hissed in the streets of London, and in March 1870 were booed when they took their places at the Olympic Theatre. Some scurrilous pamphlets were circulated, including *The Coming K----*, a parody of Alfred Tennyson's *Idylls of the King*.

Gladstone felt moved to write a cautionary letter to the Prince reminding him of some of the problems arising from the scandals that had surrounded the Prince Regent:

> The conviction of my mind, based on no short experience, is that, so long as the nation has confidence in the personal character of its Sovereign, the Throne of this Empire may be regarded as secure; but that the revival of circumstances only half a century old must tend rapidly to impair its strength and might bring about its overthrow ... and such nearness to the Throne as that of Your Royal Highness for this purpose is almost identical with its possession.

Fortunately for the Prince of Wales, fortunately for the young Prince George, the British monarchy was robust enough to survive scandal and criticism, and the British people were conservative enough to wish to preserve the institution. The relationship between Prince George's parents, though equally under stress, also showed remarkable qualities of endurance, affection and family love.

The Prince and Princess of Wales with their two sons in about 1866. Prince George is on the left and Prince Albert Victor on the right.

In all, Princess Alexandra bore her husband six children. Prince George's elder brother, Albert Victor, was eighteen months his senior. Then there were three sisters: Princess Louise, born in 1867 and declared Princess Royal in 1905; Princess Victoria, born in 1868; and Princess Maud, born in 1869 and subsequently Queen of Norway. A third boy, Alexander John, was born in 1871, but lived for only twenty-four hours.

The Prince of Wales adored his children, and was in return adored by them. His boisterous temperament, his love of company and his plain, direct use of language enabled him to communicate wonderfully with his own children and, indeed,

17

LEFT AND RIGHT
Two early photographs of
Prince George as a child.
Among the upper classes
it was fashionable for
small boys to wear girls'
clothes, whereas boys
from poor families often
wore their sisters'
clothes of necessity.

Edward, Prince of Wales, and his family. Despite their arranged marriage and the scandal of Edward's affairs, he and Alexandra made a close and affectionate family life for their children. His three daughters (from left to right) are Princess Maud, Princess Victoria and Princess Louise. Prince Albert Victor and Prince George stand to left and right of their mother.

with any children. He encouraged zestful play, even to the extent of allowing races with pieces of hot buttered toast along the stripes of his trousers. When, before his coronation in 1902, his grandchildren stared speechlessly as he stood arrayed in his finery, he remarked, 'Good morning, children. Am I not a funny-looking old man?'

Prince George held his father in some awe, despite the latter's affability, throughout his childhood. This feeling lingered on even into manhood. Yet the Prince of Wales was ready to show his second son great affection and regard, and to place enormous trust in him. Anxious to avoid the unhappy precedent of his own troubled relationship with his father, Prince Albert, the Prince of Wales attempted to foster a spirit of brotherly friendship with his own sons. It has often been claimed that the Prince of Wales and Prince George kept no secrets from each other: this is no doubt an exaggerated view, since there was clearly much in the Prince of Wales's private life that his son, with his deep devotion to his mother, Princess Alexandra, would have found unpalatable. But in the broader sense, it does seem as if father and son enjoyed an intimacy which did credit to them both.

If Prince George respected and loved his father, he was passionately devoted to his mother. Princess Alexandra aroused warm feelings in others, and Queen Victoria wrote in 1864 'Alex is really a dear, excellent, right-minded soul, whom one must dearly love and respect. I often think her lot is not an easy one, but she is very fond of Bertie [the Prince of Wales], though not blind!' Though indeed not blind, Princess Alexandra frequently found it expedient to shut her eyes to some of her husband's activities.

She was the eldest daughter of King Christian IX of Denmark. In 1863 she came to England to marry the Prince of Wales, and was heralded on her arrival as the 'Sea-King's daughter from over the sea'. Alexandra combined an extraordinary and almost unfading beauty with a simplicity of manner and a warm nature. She was notoriously unpunctual and disorderly, yet she lavished attention on her children and was unfailing in her support of certain charities and good causes, especially in the field of nursing.

To Prince George she was simply 'Darling Motherdear'. Her early influence upon his development was profound. He learned from her a straightforward belief in Christian principles, and invested in her a love of particular intensity. Hating to be parted from her, it is arguable that Prince George was emancipated from his emotional dependence on his mother only by his marriage to Princess Mary of Teck in 1893.

The prince spent his early boyhood mostly at Sandringham in Norfolk, although occasionally the family visited London, or Osborne on the Isle of Wight. At six years of age Prince George began his formal education, together with his elder brother Prince Albert Victor, known to the family as Eddy. The

Prince of Wales selected the Reverend John Dalton as tutor for his two sons. The Reverend Dalton possessed first-class academic qualifications, an orderly mind and a devotion to the best interests of his royal pupils. He instilled his own taste for tidiness and thoroughness into Prince George, though he was less successful with Prince Eddy. The Reverend Dalton's association with Prince George, as tutor, friend and Dean of Windsor, lasted until the former's death in 1931.

There was no shirking with Mr Dalton in charge. The two princes got up at seven o'clock and studied geography and English before breakfast. At eight o'clock there was either Bible study or history, and at nine either Euclid or algebra. They were then allowed an hour's break, which was followed by a Latin or French lesson until the main meal at two o'clock. There were various sporting activities in the afternoon, then tea, English, music and prep. Bedtime was at eight o'clock.

It is interesting that the Prince of Wales approved this programme as a distinct contrast to the dismal cramming he had received from his own tutor, Baron Stockmar. Neither the Stockmar method nor the Dalton method, however, was destined to produce academic high flyers, though this was hardly the purpose and was, indeed, unlikely, given the material to be worked on.

But Prince George did develop a high sense of duty and responsibility under Mr Dalton's tutelage, even though these admirable qualities were not always to the fore in the weekly journal kept by his teacher, who wrote, for the week ending 2 September 1876: 'Prince G. this week has been much troubled by silly fretfulness of temper and general spirit of contradiction. Otherwise work with me has been up to the usual average.' 23 September: 'Prince George has been good this week. He shows however too much disposition to find fault with his brother.' 14 October: 'Too fretful; and inclined to be lazy and silly this week.' 30 December: 'Prince George wants application, steady application. Though he is not deficient in a wish to progress, still his sense of self-approbation is almost the only motive power in him. He has not nearly so high a sense of right and wrong for its own sake as his elder brother.'

Mr Dalton was not alone in urging Prince George to strive for moral excellence. Queen Victoria bestowed upon her

OPPOSITE Prince George with Princess Alexandra. He was devoted to her and hated the partings from 'Darling Motherdear' which his naval career demanded.

grandsons love, kindness and, not infrequently, advice. In 1873, she gave Prince George a watch for his birthday, 'hoping that it will serve to remind you to be very punctual in everything and very exact in all your duties. . . . I hope you will be a good, obedient, truthful boy, kind to all, humble-minded, dutiful and always trying to be of use to others! Above all, God-fearing and striving always to do His Will.'

Punctuality, obedience and attention to duty were essential qualities for a successful naval officer, and in 1877 the question of the Prince's entry into the service was a matter for urgent consideration. Prince George, as the second son of the Prince of Wales, was not expected to succeed eventually to the throne. A naval career had therefore been marked out for him. It was not, however, Prince George alone who had to be considered. His brother, Prince Eddy, was a listless and backward pupil, showing little interest in the world of learning and ideas. Mr Dalton argued in a memorandum that

> Prince Albert Victor requires the stimulus of Prince George's company to induce him to work at all.... Difficult as the education of Prince Albert Victor is now, it would be doubly or trebly so if Prince George were to leave him. Prince George's lively presence is his mainstay and chief incentive to exertion; and to Prince George again, the presence of his elder brother is most wholesome as a check against that tendency to self-conceit which is apt at times to show itself in him.

Mr Dalton went on to stress that if Prince Eddy accompanied his brother to the Royal Navy training ship *Britannia*, it would encourage 'those habits of promptitude and method, of manliness and self-reliance, in which he is now somewhat deficient'.

Queen Victoria did not approve of the two princes entering the *Britannia* together, pointing out that 'their positions (if they live) will be totally *different* and it is not intended that they should *both* enter the navy.... The very rough sort of life to which boys are exposed on board ship is the very thing not calculated to make a refined and amiable Prince, who in after years (if God spares him) is to ascend to the throne.' The Queen lost this battle, even after invoking William III, Baron Stockmar, the Prince Consort (inevitably) and *History!* On 5 June 1877, Prince George passed his entrance examination for the navy. In September he joined the *Britannia*, at Dartmouth, carrying Prince Eddy and Mr Dalton in the wake of his success.

So began Prince George's lengthy association with the Royal Navy. He spent fifteen active years in the service, from 1877 to 1893, graduating from cadet to captain. Only the death of Prince Eddy in 1892 and Prince George's sudden and unexpected transformation to heir presumptive ended his naval career. These fifteen years were among the most formative of his life.

The love of order which Mr Dalton had implanted accorded neatly with the demands of naval discipline. Prince George's directness of manner and bluff simplicity were in turn prized and stimulated by life on the quarterdeck. The navy left two more outward marks upon him: one was the full beard which he sported for much of his life, the other was his habit of creasing his trousers from right to left, not back to front. These foibles are not those which cause great empires to rise and fall, but they perhaps show the permanent affection Prince George felt for nautical ways.

On board the *Britannia*, Prince George soon showed ability in mathematics and in sailing. In other ways, the training ship was a great leveller. Aristocratic, let alone royal, birth was no protection from the rigours of fagging or the risk of bullying. Seniority counted for something, strength counted for a lot more, as Prince George once recalled:

> It never did me any good to be a Prince ... and many was the time I wished I hadn't been. It was a pretty tough place and, so far from making any allowances for our disadvantages, the other boys made a point of taking it out on us on the grounds that they'd never be able to do it later on. There was a lot of fighting among the cadets and the rule was that if challenged you had to accept. So they used to make me go up and challenge the bigger boys – I was awfully small then – and I'd get a hiding time and again.
>
> Then we had a sort of tuck-shop on land ... only we weren't allowed to bring any eatables into the ship, and they used to search you as you came aboard. Well, the big boys used to fag me to bring them back a whole lot of stuff – and I was always found out and got into trouble in addition to having the stuff confiscated. And the worst of it was, it was always *my* money; they never paid me back – I suppose they thought there was plenty more where that came from, but in point of fact we were only given a shilling a week pocket money, so it meant a lot to me, I can tell you.

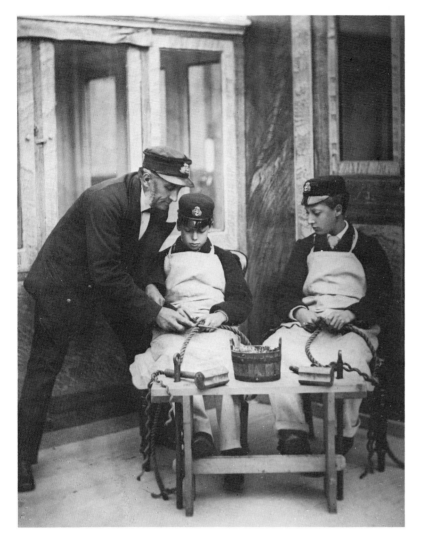

OPPOSITE Prince George (left) and Prince Albert Victor, known to the family as Eddy, in front of the training ship *Britannia* at Dartmouth. They were sent together into the navy, despite Queen Victoria's opposition, so that Prince George's 'lively presence' would encourage the slow Prince Eddy to greater efforts.

LEFT The two Princes as cadets in about 1877.

The Royal Navy fancied itself a more democratic service than the Army. Prince George's bloody nose and confiscated pocket money were hardly the symbols of an innate social superiority, and the warm cossetting of 'Motherdear' was as far away as the solid presence of grandmama. But Prince George survived, and passed out of the *Britannia* in 1879 at the age of fourteen.

Although Dartmouth had broadened horizons that had previously been circumscribed by Sandringham and Osborne, the two Princes still lacked any first-hand contact with the wider world. When Prince George's time on the *Britannia* was drawing to a close, it had been agreed that he should undertake a lengthy cruise on a navy training-ship. But the problem of Prince Eddy's dormant intellect once more presented itself. Mr Dalton again advocated that the elder brother should accompany the younger, and thus draw support from the relationship. It would certainly have been inadvisable to isolate Prince Eddy's backwardness in the demanding and not always kindly environment of a public school.

So Prince Eddy and, after a show of reluctance, Mr Dalton, accompanied Prince George on the world cruise of HMS *Bacchante*. It was no light matter to commit the two sons of the Prince of Wales to the perils of the sea; the Cabinet condemned the plan, and the Prime Minister, Benjamin Disraeli, informed Queen Victoria that he could not 'adequately describe the feelings of Your Majesty's Ministers on the subject'. But the Queen adamantly approved of the joint venture, Disraeli let himself be persuaded and, in September 1879, the *Bacchante* sailed from Spithead.

Between 1879 and 1882 the *Bacchante* undertook three cruises, and the two Princes visited the Mediterranean, the West Indies, Ireland, Spain, South America, South Africa, Australia, Japan, China, Singapore and Egypt. Prince George served as a midshipman, though excused the night watch and boat service in foul weather. Prince Eddy's main task was to continue his studies under the worthy Mr Dalton. Unfortunately he made only faltering progress, while Prince George passed his midshipman's exams with ease.

The first cruise of the *Bacchante* took the Princes to some of the bastions of British naval power in the Mediterranean, as well as to the impoverished but beautiful islands of the West Indies. In Gibraltar the Governor, Lord Napier, mistaking Prince Eddy's slowness for a profoundly contemplative nature, wrote, 'The youngest is the most lively and popular, but I think the eldest is better suited to his situation – he is shy and not demonstrative, but does the right things as a young gentleman in a quiet way.'

In Barbados, a journalist mistook a temporary dusting of pollen on the Princes' faces for tattoo marks, and so began the scandal of the 'tattooed royal nose'. Princess Alexandra chided Prince George, asking him why he had got his 'impudent snout

HMS *Bacchante* leaving Portland harbour with the Princes aboard in 1879.

tattooed? What an *object* you must look, and won't everybody
stare at the ridiculous boy with an anchor on his nose?' However
the truth was soon revealed, and the British nation was thus
denied its first King-Emperor with a tattooed nose.

The Princes' second cruise was short and uneventful, but in
September 1880 the *Bacchante* set out on a third voyage, which
was to last for two years. For Prince George it meant that the
apron strings which still connected him with his mother would
be stretched to breaking-point. On the point of departure he
wrote 'My darling Motherdear, I miss you so very much & felt
so sorry when I had to say goodbye to you and sisters.... I felt
so miserable yesterday saying goodbye. I shall think of you all
going to Scotland tonight and I only wish we were going
too.... *So goodbye darling Motherdear, dearest Papa & sisters.*'

By the end of the year the *Bacchante* had reached South

LEFT The Zulu King
Cetewayo in detention at
Cape Town Castle after
defeat in the Zulu War
of 1879. The engraving
is titled 'Cetewayo
Civilised'.

OPPOSITE The retreat
from Majuba Hill in
February 1881 during the
Transvaal War.

America, a continent upon which the Union Jack scarcely flew, but one much affected by British investment and exports. In January 1881, while anchored in the Falkland Islands, however, the naval squadron of which the *Bacchante* was part was ordered to sail post-haste for the Cape of Good Hope. The Union Jack did fly over the colony of the Cape, and also over Natal. Since 1877 it had also fluttered uncertainly over the ex-republic of the Transvaal, which Disraeli had been persuaded to annex in order to further European security and British interests in southern Africa. But the Afrikaners of the Transvaal, sons of those Cape Dutch who had trekked away from British authority in the 1830s, had grown impatient with the annexation. The Zulu menace on the Transvaal's borders had been thwarted, but the Gladstone administration which took office in 1880 seemed no more willing than the outgoing Tory ministry to implement internal self-government.

So the Transvaalers rose in revolt, and it was to help quell this threat, rather than to deal with 'the Basuter disturbances' (as Prince George put it), that the *Bacchante*'s squadron left the Falkland Islands. This frantic dash across the Atlantic was of no avail, for within ten days of the squadron's arrival at the Cape, the Transvaalers overwhelmed a British force at Majuba Hill, killing the commanding officer, General Colley, in the process. Prince George made his own judgment on these momentous events in a letter to his mother, remarking, 'This is really a dredful war is it not? All these poor people killed & also poor General Colley.'

Despite Queen Victoria's fears that her two grandsons would somehow get physically involved in the hostilities, and the Prince of Wales's hope that they *would* see some fighting, their most exciting experiences during the *Bacchante*'s stay at Cape Town were probably a visit to an ostrich farm and to chief Cetewayo. The latter was the defeated King of the Zulus who had been interned near Cape Town. Prince George was much impressed by this fallen heir of the legendary Chaka, recording in his diary that 'He himself is eighteen stone and his wives 16 & 17 stone; there are four of them, they are very fine women, all over six feet.'

When the *Bacchante* sailed from Cape Town in April 1881, the Gladstone government was negotiating the Transvaal's independence with the resolute Paul Kruger, the new power in the land. Prince George had not, however, heard the last of South Africa where, within two decades, there was to be a far more cataclysmic eruption of Anglo-Afrikaner hostility.

Leaving behind them a troubled portion of the empire, the two Princes now headed for Australia where loyalty to the British Crown was remarkably solid, if not universal. Four hundred miles from the Australian coast, the *Bacchante*'s rudder was badly damaged in heavy seas and it was only after desperate repairs, and much heart-searching by Mr Dalton, that the ship anchored safely off Western Australia. Fairly brisk visits to Sydney and Brisbane followed, and then the cruise swept Prince George and Prince Eddy to Fiji, Japan, Hong Kong, Shanghai, Singapore, Colombo, Egypt, Palestine and Greece. In Japan they were received at the formal and tradition-conscious Court of the Mikado, and in Greece, with hilarious informality, by their uncle and aunt the King and Queen of the Hellenes. On 5 August 1882, the *Bacchante* docked at Cowes, on the Isle of Wight, and the Prince and Princess of Wales took their sons to greet their grandmother at Osborne. 'Georgie', wrote Queen Victoria, 'is much grown. He has still the same bright, merry face as ever.'

Prince George had gained more than a few extra inches from his two years at sea. Although Mr Dalton noted that his 'excitable temperament... still sometimes leads him to fret at difficulties instead of facing them', generally his educational progress had been very satisfactory. Vagaries of spelling remained, but when the *Bacchante*'s rudder had been smashed it was Mr Dalton who had fretted at the difficulty while Prince George had viewed the accident with nautical calm. Nor, despite George's 'excitable temperament', did a fellow-midshipman ever remember his losing his temper.

The spartan life at sea, the naval demands of discipline and common sense, the tolerance and goodfellowship required in the mess-room, and a voyage round the world, all provided appropriate experience for a young Prince who was eventually to reign when the British Empire reached its territorial zenith.

2
Sailor Prince and Heir Presumptive 1882-1901

IN 1883 PRINCE GEORGE was appointed a midshipman in HMS *Canada*. This vessel was part of the West Indian and North American squadron, which was not the detachment of the navy most likely to be hurled against some foreign foe, and which was, indeed, scrapped during Admiral Fisher's naval reforms which began in 1903. The appointment to the *Canada* separated Prince George from Prince Eddy for the first time in their lives. Prince Eddy stayed at home to be heavily coached for entrance to Cambridge University, while Prince George lived the plain life of a midshipman who was 'to be treated in all respects and on all occasions, while on board ship, in the same manner as the other officers of his own rank with whom he is serving'. Prince Eddy seems to have missed his brother acutely; it is not certain that Prince George was similarly affected.

In the autumn of 1884 Prince George spent six months at the Royal Naval College at Greenwich, followed by a gunnery course on HMS *Excellent* at Portsmouth. He won glowing reports at Portsmouth and, more significantly, gained first-class marks in gunnery, torpedo work and seamanship. In October 1885, the First Lord of the Admiralty, Lord George Hamilton, told the Prince's delighted father that 'the capacity which Prince George has shown is unusual'. The Prince now attained the rank of lieutenant, and seemed set fair for a naval career that would rest at least as much on his innate ability as on his royal birth.

Prince George was now twenty years of age, and without any immediate prospect of an appropriate marriage. Queen Victoria, having watched her own eldest son march firmly down the primrose path of dalliance, urged her grandson to tread more carefully. In June 1885 she wrote, in tones reminiscent of Polonius:

> Avoid the many evil temptations wh. beset *all* young men and especially Princes. Beware of flatterers, too great love of amusement, of *races* & betting & playing high. I hear on all sides what a good steady boy you are & how you can be trusted. Still you must always be on the watch & must not fear ridicule if you do what is right.
>
> Alas! Society is very bad these days; what is wrong is winked at, allowed even, & as for betting or anything of that kind, no end of young and older men have been ruined, parents hearts broken, &

PREVIOUS PAGES
Prince George with
a naval group in 1888.

Prince George in mufti. Despite the fears of Queen Victoria that he would take after his father, his leisure activities were most respectable.

great names and Titles dragged in the dirt. It is in your power to do immense good by setting an example & keeping your dear Grandpapa's name before you.

Prince George's relaxations were unlikely to break the hearts of parents, grandparents or, indeed, anyone else. While serving in the Mediterranean between 1886 and 1888, his principal pastimes were stamp-collecting, polo, a game or two of billiards and visiting the family of his uncle the Duke of Edinburgh, who was currently commander-in-chief of the

Mediterranean fleet. He also grew a beard. His brother Eddy, outpaced in so many other fields, now found himself an also-ran in the matter of facial hair. In December 1886, he wrote to Prince George, 'Oh yes, I got your photos all right and thought them very good, but would have preferred you without a beard. I dare say it is more comfortable than shaving, which I now do nearly every day, but it makes you look so much older and I think you might take it off before you come home, if you feel inclined to. Old Curzon has taken his off and looks very much better.'

Prince George was in his early twenties when he began his service in the Mediterranean, but his emotional dependence on his family was enormous. After meeting his father at Cannes in March 1886 he wrote 'I cannot tell you how much I miss you every minute of the day.... I felt so very low at saying goodbye to you.' A few months later he told his mother 'You will be going to Sandringham almost at once I suppose for dear Papa's birthday. How I wish I was going to be there too, it almost makes me cry when I think of it. I wonder who will have that sweet little room of mine, you must go and see it sometimes and imagine that your little Georgie dear is living in it.'

Queen Victoria's children and grandchildren set a high price on family love, tinged, as it so often was, with mawkish sentimentality and expressions of cloying sweetness. Princess Alexandra had added the further ingredient of passionate and possessive mother-love. Somewhat isolated by the awkward predicaments of her married life, and also by the deafness which afflicted her middle years, she clung to her children for sustenance and support. Perhaps, in the process, she drained them of a certain amount of independence, and held back their emotional development.

Prince George exchanged letters of great intensity with his mother. In 1888 he told her, from Naples, 'In about three weeks' time I shall be leaving here for beloved old England again, it seems too delightful to be true and then in about a month's time I shall see your beloved lovely face once more. Oh! Won't I give it a great big kiss and shan't we have lots to tell one another darling Motherdear after having been separated for these long 7 months!' At the end of 1889 Princess Alexandra wrote, 'I must write these few lines... to tell you...

Princess Alexandra (second
from left) looking scarcely
older than her three daughters
Princess Maud (left), Princess
Louise (centre) and Princess
Victoria, who is lighting
Prince George's cigarette.

how dreadfully I missed you for Xmas. There were all the tables [containing Christmas presents] excepting yrs. & there were all their cheery voices excepting the cheeriest of all & yr. bright little face with its turned-up snout oh I did miss it & really shed a little secret tear for my Georgie dear!'

In addition to maintaining these endearing yet childish exchanges with her twenty-four-year-old son, the Princess of Wales fed him political opinions of an extraordinarily partial and naïve nature. As a Danish princess, she hated Prussia for the invasion of the duchies of Schleswig and Holstein in 1864. She also loathed Bismarck, whom she saw as the instigator of that brief war against her father, King Christian IX. When the Emperor Frederick III of Germany died of cancer only ninety-nine days after ascending the throne in 1888, Princess Alexandra accused the new Kaiser William II of insulting behaviour towards his mother, the widowed Empress Frederick.

In 1890, Prince George accompanied his father on a state visit to Berlin, and his cousin William II made him the honorary commander of a Prussian regiment. Princess Alexandra was incensed, and wrote an impassioned letter to her son:

> And so, my Georgie boy has become a real live filthy bluecoated Picklehaube German soldier!!! Well, I never thought to have lived to see *that*! But never mind; as you say, it could not have been helped – it was your misfortune and not your fault – and anything was better – even my two boys being sacrificed!!! – than Papa being made a German Admiral – that I could not have survived – you would have had to look for your poor old Motherdear at the bottom of the sea, the first time he adorned himself with it [sic]!

It would be a mistake to rate Princess Alexandra's political influence at all high. Even Queen Victoria, who held strong opinions on many matters of foreign and domestic policy, was powerless to deflect her ministers from their chosen course. Still, Princess Alexandra's dedicated distrust and dislike of the German Empire doubtless contributed a little to the strained relationship which persisted between the Prince of Wales and his flamboyant nephew the Kaiser.

Fortunately, the British and German Empires were not likely to embark on total war to avenge some slight, real or imaginary, that had been suffered by a member of their respective royal houses. British foreign policy in the 1880s wished to steer clear of the entanglements of foreign alliances and foreign wars. International peace and free trade were the twin aims of both Liberal and Conservative governments. The Royal Navy supervised Britain's world-wide interests, and put petty foreign potentates in their place if need be.

Lord Salisbury had not yet coined the phrase 'splendid isolation', but that was already a fair description of Britain's position. This isolation was apparently rendered more secure by the existence of the British Empire. Superficially, the Empire ensured Britain's great power status. In fact, Britain was a world power that had also acquired a huge Empire. The mainspring of British supremacy was not the possession of Ashanti-land or Bengal, nor the support of the self-governing colonies such as Queensland or Canada, it was rather to be found in the flying start that Britain had made in the process of industrialisation. It was British exports that were irresistible, not the collective wisdom of British statesmen, or the marshalled strength of the British Empire.

Nonetheless, imperialism was soon to become a fashionable political philosophy, and the Empire would generate immense optimism as well as provoke persistent criticism. In 1887 Prince George attended Queen Victoria's Golden Jubilee, which was made the occasion for assembling imperial representatives in London and, incidentally, for holding the first Colonial Conference. He remained devoted to the Empire until his death, and his life-time encompassed the aftermath of the Indian Mutiny, the Victorian imperial high noon and the beginning of the end with the passing of the Government of India Act in 1935.

By 1890, however, Prince George had no notion that his career was to involve anything more than a steady advancement in the Royal Navy. In 1889, he had undertaken his first independent command, Torpedo Boat No. 79, and soon distinguished himself by rescuing another crippled torpedo boat in heavy seas. In 1890 he was made Commander of the first-class gunboat HMS *Thrush* and served in the West Indian and North American squadron.

Apart from his career, marriage seemed the only other possible commitment. Queen Victoria, who had found such solace in wedlock, urged both Prince Eddy and Prince George to marry. In February 1891 the latter sent her an artless reply on the subject:

> I quite agree with you, dearest Grandmama & understand your reason for wishing Eddy & I to marry as soon as possible. But still I think marrying too young is a bad thing.... Then again the wife ought not to be too young; look at the poor Crown Prince Rudolph. She was certainly too young when he married her; she became very ill after her first child was born & he was naturally a very wild young man. The result was he committed suicide & killed this poor girl & brought the most terrible sorrow & shame to his poor wife & parents; that is only one instance of young marriages that I know of.

As it happened, the matrimonial prospects of Prince George and his brother were soon to undergo convulsions as terrible as those described above, though infinitely more respectable. In November 1891, while both princes were at Sandringham after their father's birthday celebrations, Prince George contracted typhoid. The royal family had good cause to dread typhoid, for this disease had carried off the Prince Consort in 1861 and had threatened the life of the Prince of Wales ten years later. The poet Alfred Austin had written a remarkable piece of verse during the Prince of Wales's illness. It contained two immortal lines:

> Flash'd from his bed, the electric tidings came,
> He is not better; he is much the same.

However, the Prince of Wales had pulled through. So did Prince George, after struggling for life for two weeks. While he was convalescing at Sandringham, the engagement of his brother, Prince Eddy, the Duke of Clarence, to Princess Mary (or May) of Teck was announced. But on 7 January 1892, Prince Eddy fell ill with influenza, which was then a potent and justly feared disease. Influenza developed into pneumonia, and on 14 January the heir presumptive died.

Prince George was deeply shocked by his brother's death. He had attended him with complete devotion as he lay dying. Subsequently he told Queen Victoria, 'I am sure no two brothers could have loved each other more than we did. Alas! it is only now that I have found out how deeply I did love him.'

Prince Eddy, the Duke of Clarence, who was to have married Princess Mary.

The nation participated whole-heartedly in the grief of the royal family, and a popular ballad was composed, with the following chorus:

> A nation wrapped in mourning,
> Shed bitter tears today,
> For the noble Duke of Clarence,
> And fair young Princess May.

Looked at more dispassionately, the death of Prince Eddy was not without its advantages for the continuing viability of the British monarchy. The dead Prince had failed to exhibit much aptitude for his career in the army; he hated military routine and thought his first commanding officer a lunatic. But then he had failed to exhibit much aptitude for anything, except, perhaps, what Victorian moralists were wont to call 'dissipation'. Women stirred Prince Eddy to some level of activity. Unfortunately such activities were not sufficient occupation in themselves for a future monarch of the greatest power in the world.

Prince George was certainly not dissipated. His private life was conventional and straight-forward, even dull. But his reliability, good sense, shrewdness and anxiety to please were, in their royal context, admirable qualities. Queen Victoria, at any rate, valued them highly. It only remained to give him a ducal title, and to find him a wife.

Both were close at hand. In May 1892, Prince George became Duke of York, Earl of Inverness and Baron Killarney. Queen Victoria did not like the revival of the dukedom of York because of its association with her notorious uncle, the second son of George III. But, on 17 June, the new Duke of York took his seat in the House of Lords. 'Fancy,' wrote Princess Alexandra, 'my Georgie boy doing that and now being a grand old Duke of York!'

A year after acquiring his dukedom, Prince George also acquired a wife. Princess Mary had been left delicately stranded by the premature death of Prince Eddy. Not for the first time in the history of the British monarchy, it seemed appropriate for a younger sibling to take the bride originally destined for his elder brother. The precedent of Prince Arthur, Henry VIII and Catherine of Aragon was not a particularly happy one, but at least, with the evident fertility of the House of Saxe-Coburg-Gotha, there was no need to anticipate an anxious search for an heir to the throne.

Other brides had been suggested for Prince George. There was Princess Marie, daughter of Queen Victoria's second son Alfred, Duke of Edinburgh, and known in the family as 'Missy'. Clever, conceited and melodramatic, 'Missy' would have made a restless future Queen of England. Happily, she chose instead to marry Ferdinand, Prince of Hohenzollern-Sigmaringen, and ended up as a restless Queen of Romania. Then there was

OPPOSITE
Princess Mary of Teck.

Princess Helena Victoria of Schleswig-Holstein, known in the family as 'Snipe' because of her long nose. Prince George's mother had a low opinion of this potential bride, as, indeed, of most others: 'So', she wrote '[Prince and Princess Christian of Schleswig-Holstein] have been following you about with their lovely Snipe! Well it *will* be a pleasure to welcome that beauty as yr bride – when may we expect the news? You see she is quite prepared to take you by storm by already offering you her contrafeit [picture] in a frame!!'

Princess Mary's nose was of admirable proportions, however, and she was, in general, a comely young woman. She was the daughter of the Duke of Teck, and, on her mother's side, great-grandaughter of King George III. She had been born at Kensington Palace in 1867, and had lived most of her life in Britain. Her manner was rather reserved and careful, and she possessed a fine memory and well-developed powers of observation. She was very well educated, and deeply interested in history, particularly family history. She also developed a taste for assessing and accumulating works of art, and had built up a fine collection by the time of her death. Some thought her too serious, and Queen Victoria's eldest daughter, the widowed Empress Frederick, wrote, a year after Prince Eddy's death:

> May is … still all in black of course, but she seemed to me a little stiff & cold! I hear her praised on all sides…. She is certainly very nice in manner – etc. but I do not think she has much charm or is very fascinating! She may have been shy with me seeing me again after all this sorrow! and it is a shy and difficult position for her – as the newspapers are perpetually talking of her Betrothal to Georgie.

Queen Victoria, however, was an enthusiastic supporter of Princess Mary's qualities, and Prince George, knowing of his father's warm approval for the match, prepared to abandon his bachelorhood. Early in May 1893, he and Princess Mary visited Sheen Lodge, the home of his sister Princess Louise, who set the formalities in motion by saying 'Now, Georgie, don't you think you ought to take May into the garden to look at the frogs in the pond?' The frogs did the trick, and the next day the engagement was announced.

Prince George's royal grandmother wrote to congratulate him: 'Let me now say how thankful I am that this great and so long & ardently wished for event is settled…. Say everything affectionate to dear May, for whom this must be a *trying moment* full of such mixed feelings. But she cannot find a *better* husband than you and I am sure she will be a good, devoted and useful wife to you.'

Princess Alexandra reacted honestly to the prospect of losing her only remaining son to another woman. Prior to the engagement she had written, 'Indeed it is sad to think we shall never be able to be together and travel in the same way – yet there is a bond of love between us, that of mother and child, which nothing can ever diminish or render less binding – and nobody can, or ever shall, come between me and my darling Georgie boy.'

Prince George and Princess Mary were married in the Chapel Royal, St James's Palace, on 6 July 1893. It was a relief to both bride and groom that the tense and taxing period of preparation for the wedding was now over. Princess Mary had told her fiancé, 'I know I am always losing my temper with somebody or something & I assure you this is not generally the case.... This is a simply *horrid* time we are going through & I am only looking forward to the time when you & I shall be alone at Sandringham.' The Duke of York replied 'Thank God we both understand each other, & I think it really unnecessary for me to tell you how deep my love for you my darling is & I feel is growing stronger & stronger every time I see you; although I may appear shy and cold. But this worry & busy time is most annoying, & when we do meet it is only to talk business.'

The wedding day was hot and noisy, and a great success. Huge crowds assembled to cheer not only the bride and groom, but also Queen Victoria, a shy, diminutive figure almost submerged in the roar of her subjects' acclamation. Then there was Princess Alexandra, wan, wistful and beautiful; the Duchess of Teck, Princess Mary's mother, revelling in her greatest day; and, among the representatives of foreign powers, the Tsarevitch Nicholas, looking unbelievably like his cousin Prince George.

At last it was all over, and the nervous bridegroom and the reserved bride faced each other as a honeymoon couple in 'York Cottage', a modest residence in the grounds of Sandringham. The first week of the honeymoon was beset with thunderstorms, which frightened Princess Mary, and hindered outside expeditions. For Prince George, the chaff of the quarterdeck

'She cannot find a better husband than you'

OVERLEAF The wedding of Prince George, now Duke of York, and Princess Mary in the Chapel Royal, St James's Palace in 1893. The Duchess of Teck, the bride's mother, sits in the foreground to the right, and opposite her is Queen Victoria.

York Cottage, in the grounds of Sandringham, where the young couple spent their honeymoon and many years of married life. The house was so small for the growing family of children, nannies and secretaries that the Duke of York once remarked that he supposed the servants must sleep in the trees.

and the adulation of 'Motherdear' must have seemed very far away; for Princess Mary, her husband's lack of profound cultural or intellectual interests may have proved a trial. But they managed. They played cards, and rearranged furniture, and read Greville's *Memoirs* to each other.

Being of an independent mind, despite the Empress Frederick's scathing judgment that 'All her thoughts, views and ideas appear to me to be rather banal, commonplace and conventional', Princess Mary probably resented her early lack of freedom in dealing with domestic matters. York Cottage had been fully furnished before the wedding by Prince George and a 'man from Maples', whose tastes Princess Mary did not necessarily share. Then there was the proximity of Motherdear at the big house. A few months after their wedding Prince

50

George wrote to tell his bride, 'Motherdear, sisters & Charlotte [Knollys] lunched with me today.... Mama afterwards moved the furniture in the drawing room, which certainly gives ever so much more room, & I think looks much prettier, of course if you don't like it ... we can move it all back again in a minute.' Princess Mary replied, with considerable restraint, 'I am so glad "Motherdear" tried to arrange our drawing room, she has so much taste ... only I thought that as the Scotch furniture had not come, it was scarcely worth while to waste a lot of time arranging it when [it will] have to be changed.'

Princess Mary's desire to read a good deal, and her serious attempts to 'improve her mind', also jarred with the more hedonistic and raffish pursuits of the Prince of Wales's set at the big house. Still, the man who mattered most found himself increasingly enamoured of his bride, and some months after the marriage Prince George wrote:

> You know by this time that I never do anything by halves, when I asked you to marry me, I was very fond of you, but not very much in love with you, but I saw in *you* the person I was capable of loving most deeply, if you only returned that love.... I have tried to understand you & to know you, & with the happy result that I know now that I do *love* you darling girl with all my heart, & am simply *devoted* to you.... *I adore you sweet May.*

In June 1894, less than a year after the marriage of the Duke and Duchess of York, their first child was born. The baby boy was later to become Prince of Wales, King Edward VIII and finally Duke of Windsor. Like his father before him, Prince George had to wrestle with Queen Victoria's opinions on names. She wrote, 'I am *most anxious naturally* that he should bear the name of his beloved Great Grandfather, a name which brought untold blessings to the whole Empire & that *Albert* should be his 1st name.'

> My Darling Grandmama [replied Prince George], You have always shown me the greatest possible kindness.... & ever since I can remember I have always tried my best to be a dutiful grandson to you & never go against your wishes. Long before our dear child was born, both May and I settled that if it was a boy we should call him Edward after darling *Eddy. This is the dearest wish of our hearts,* dearest Grandmama, for Edward is indeed a *sacred* name to us ... of course we intend that one of his names *shall* be *Albert.*

The York Family

Prince Edward, later Edward VIII, was the first child born to the Duke and Duchess of York. He is seen in 1894 with his father (BELOW LEFT) and a year later with Princess Mary (BELOW RIGHT). Prince Albert (RIGHT) was born in 1895 on the anniversary of the Prince Consort's death and named after him.

FAR RIGHT Queen Victoria with her great-grandchildren: Prince Edward (standing) Princess Victoria and Prince Albert (sitting), and Prince Henry in the Queen's arms.

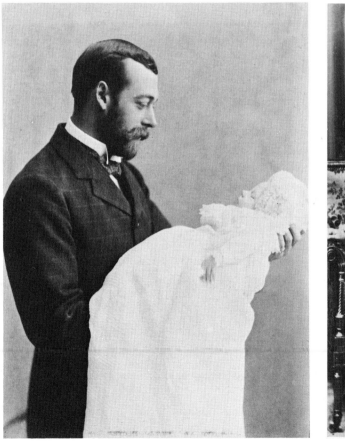

Queen Victoria responded somewhat grudgingly, 'Of course if you wish Edward to be the first name I shall not object, only I think you write as if *Edward* was the *real* name of dear Eddy, while it was *Albert Victor*.' The new Prince was eventually christened Edward Albert Christian George Andrew Patrick David. Appropriately for a future Prince of Wales, he was called David by his family and friends.

A year and a half later, in December 1895, a second son was born. Unfortunately he chose to enter the world on the mournful anniversary of the day that the Prince Consort had departed it. To soften this blow, the Duke of York asked Queen Victoria to be godmother to the baby prince, who was to bear the first name of Albert. Queen Victoria was much gratified, and wrote, 'Most gladly do I accept being Godmother to this dear little boy, born on the day his beloved Great Grandfather entered on an even greater life. He will be specially dear to me. I thank you lovingly for your kind letter & will write again soon, but I must end now to save the post. V.R.I.'

Prince Albert, so happily named, was to become King George VI. Four other children were born to the Duke and Duchess of York: in 1897, Princess Mary, later proclaimed the Princess Royal; in 1900, Prince Henry, subsequently made Duke of Gloucester; in 1902, Prince George, later created Duke of Kent. Lastly there was Prince John who was born in 1905, but who developed epilepsy and consequently lived separated from the rest of the family; he died in 1919.

So, in the latter years of the nineteenth century, as Queen Victoria's long reign was drawing to its close, the family life of the Duke and Duchess of York was flourishing. Their public life, too, was a great success. Prince George was losing his nervousness of speaking in public, and Princess Mary, with her surer grasp of language, was helping him compose his speeches. In 1897, the couple visited Ireland and were so enthusiastically received that the Prime Minister, Lord Salisbury, told Prince George that 'The devotion to your person which you have inspired is not only a result gratifying to yourself... but it will have a most valuable effect upon public feeling in Ireland, and may do much to restore the loyalty which during the last half century has been so much shaken in many districts.'

This proved an over-optimistic assessment of the Irish

A reasonably benevolent cartoon of two ardent imperialists, big K and little K.

K, k.

Men of different trades and sizes
Here you see before your eyeses:
Lanky sword and stumpy pen,
Doing useful things for men;
When the Empire wants a stitch in her
Send for Kipling and for Kitchener.

(11)

OPPOSITE Social unrest
was one of several
shadows over the
closing years of
Victoria's reign.

question. Indeed, as the century ended, events conspired to shake British complacency. The Royal Navy, for so long unchallenged, had to face the prospect of the rapid development of a large and up-to-date German navy. The German Navy Laws of 1898 and 1900 meant that the German Empire, the proud possessor of the world's finest army, would now build a fine navy as well. Numerically, the Royal Navy was still more powerful than the combined strength of the next two largest navies in the world – but for how long would this happy position now last?

Britain had also suffered an unwelcome challenge to her hitherto effortless promotion of her imperial interests. Beginning in the 1880s and reaching a crescendo in the 1890s, imperial rivalries were worked out in Africa, the Pacific, China and South-East Asia. The irruption of parvenu imperialist powers like Germany and Italy was at best irritating and inconvenient, at worst threatening. Under pressure from these new powers, and wishing to consolidate her existing interests and to protect her trade routes to India and the East, Britain had been hustled into a more active role in the partition of Africa than she might otherwise have played.

The scramble for tropical Africa had raised few qualms of conscience among the British public. After all, it was widely supposed that Europe had a duty to civilise Africa – even at the point of a bayonet. Kipling put this opinion clearly when he wrote:

> We broke a King, and we built a road,
> A court-house stands where the regiment go'ed
> And the river's clean where the red blood flowed.

But when Britain went to war with the two Afrikaner republics of the Transvaal and the Orange Free State in October 1899, the outcome was less satisfactory. The great Boer War of 1899–1902 was an apparently unequal contest between two small states that could put some 45,000 amateur soldiers in the field, and the mighty British Empire that sent 450,000 troops to South Africa. The war was fought to assert British supremacy in southern Africa, and especially to guarantee that the gold-mining industry of the Rand in the Transvaal would remain in British hands. But the struggle was not quick or cheap; it took Britain

CHAIRMAN OF No. 8 PLATFORM.

THE PROCESSION ENTERING THE PARK.

ONE OF THE SPEAKERS.

READING THE RESOLUTION.

PUTTING THE RESOLUTION TO THE VOTE.

SKETCHES AT
THE GREAT LABOUR
DEMONSTRATION
IN HYDE PARK,
SUNDAY, MAY 3.

JOHN BURNS GIVES SOME STATISTICS.

A YOUNG FORESTER.

Queen Victoria
'grandmother of Europe'
surrounded by some of her
numerous family in the
garden at Osborne. The
group includes the Duke
and Duchess of York with
their three elder children,
Prince Arthur of
Connaught, the
Battenberg Princes, and
Princess Helena Victoria of
Schleswig-Holstein.

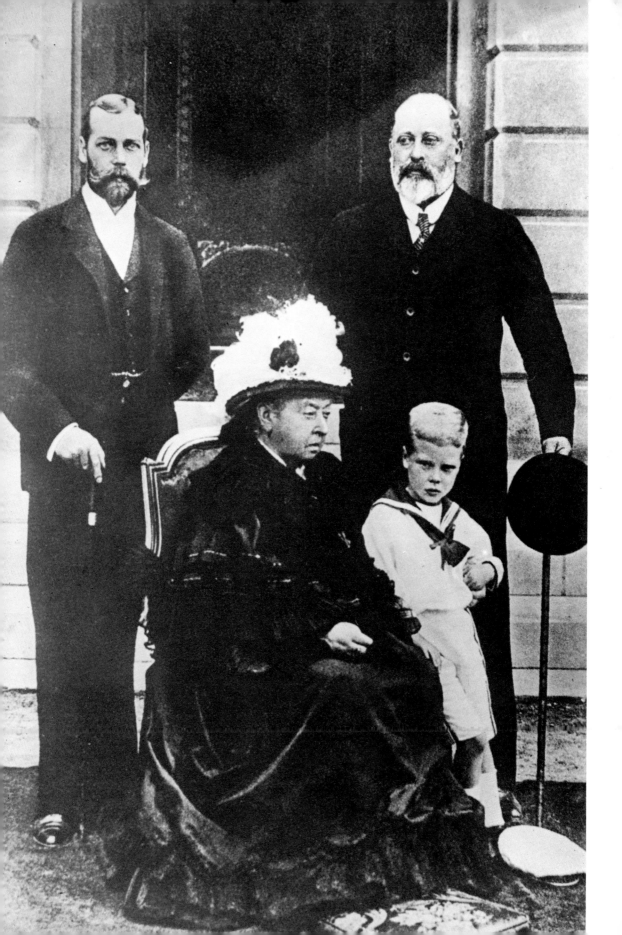

nearly three years to subdue the Afrikaners, and in the process turbulent emotions were released.

OPPOSITE Four generations of British sovereigns: Queen Victoria, Edward VII (as Prince of Wales) George V (as Duke of York) and Edward VIII (as Prince Edward of York).

Within British society there was a large section of opinion that disliked the war. In Europe there was violent feeling against Britain's alleged aggression in South Africa, and delight at the early humiliation of British arms. In April 1900, the Duke of York had to visit Berlin for the coming of age of the Crown Prince William: 'It is certainly very disagreeable to me,' he wrote, 'having to go to Berlin just now & in fact anywhere abroad as they apparently all hate us like poison.' A few boos echoed through the streets of Berlin on the Duke's arrival. It was a chastening experience to set against the earlier plaudits in Ireland.

Britain was pilloried by international opinion during the disastrous early months of the Boer War, making 'splendid isolation' seem less splendid and, in fact, embarrassingly costly. But the poor military performance in South Africa had for some time been echoed by disappointments in British industry and commerce. The great days of mid-Victorian economic supremacy were over. New industrialised nations, like the United States and Germany, were employing fresh techniques of production, and out-selling British exports in previously safe markets. At home, labour disputes and the clamour for social reform gave notice that progress was badly needed in these areas too.

The last years of Queen Victoria's reign, therefore, were troubled ones, despite the thump and glitter and splendour of the Diamond Jubilee in 1897. Almost as if to acknowledge that a new age was dawning, the old Queen died on 22 January 1901, surrounded by her family, including her distraught grandson the German Kaiser. The Prince of Wales at last entered into his long delayed inheritance, and the position of his son underwent equally important changes.

3 Prince of Wales
1901-10

PREVIOUS PAGES:
The families of Edward VII
and Tsar Nicholas II,
which were related in two
ways: Queen Alexandra's
sister was the Tsar's
mother and Edward's
sister was the Tsarina's
mother. The striking
resemblance between the
Tsar (holding cane) and
George, Duke of York
(right) sometimes caused
confusion on ceremonial
occasions.
Back row: Prince Edward
of York, Queen
Alexandra, Princess Mary
of York, Princess Victoria,
two daughters of the Tsar.
Seated: Duchess of York,
Tsar Nicholas, Edward VII,
Tsarina, Duke of York,
daughter of the Tsar.
The haemophiliac heir to
the Russian throne is
sitting on the ground
with another sister.

OPPOSITE A cartoon
on the amusements of
Edward VII published in
Munich in 1901. The
caption translated reads:
'Aren't you going to
South Africa?' 'No, I
must comfort the
widows and wives'.

THE ACCESSION OF King Edward VII blew away the cobwebs which had accumulated round the throne of Queen Victoria. The day after his mother's death he jettisoned his first name, and announced that he would be known as King Edward. Even as the new monarch busied himself with details of Queen Victoria's funeral, servants were beginning to spring-clean the royal residences. At Windsor, Eastern trophies were found infested with moths, and tons of ivory were discovered rotting in an attic.

Lord Esher, although a close personal friend of the new King, regretted the passing of the 'mystery and awe of the old Court'. But many were delighted that Edward seemed set on establishing a Court life to rival that of Charles II. On his accession, however, the *Times* had commented that he had been 'importuned by temptation in its most seductive form', and although he had 'never failed in his duty to the throne and the nation ... we shall not pretend that there is nothing in his long career which those who respect and admire him would wish otherwise'.

But for the bulk of his subjects, King Edward's zest, forcefulness and human weaknesses were refreshing qualities. His social life remained as active as ever. He continued to smoke one small cigar and two cigarettes before breakfast, and twelve huge cigars and twenty cigarettes during the day. He ate so heartily and voraciously that Queen Alexandra called his appetite 'terrible'. Whereas Queen Victoria had shied from the public gaze, King Edward positively sought it out. His indefatigable yachting, racegoing, theatre-going and socialising were bound to bring him into contact with his subjects, though chiefly with the better-heeled among them. Some of his female subjects even became his mistresses – a far cry from the monogamous deportment of Queen Victoria and Albert the Good. Hillaire Belloc celebrated the activities of Edward's fast set in an unpublished, and unpublishable, ballad which included the verses:

> There will be bridge and booze 'till after three,
> And, after that, a lot of them will grope
> Along the corridors in *robes de nuit,*
> Pyjamas, or some other kind of dope.
> A sturdy matron will be set to cope
> With Lord ——, who isn't 'quite the thing',
> And give his wife the leisure to elope,
> And Mrs James will entertain the King!

King Edward loved to play the country squire at Sandringham and his pleasure in the estate was shared by his children and grandchildren.

ABOVE The King on his favourite pony leaving the house.
OPPOSITE His grandchildren Edward and Albert help to dig the new reservoir.

Edward VII was thoroughly experienced in the ways of the world, yet almost unbelievably inexperienced in matters of statecraft. Queen Victoria had jealously guarded her position as sovereign, and had failed to introduce her son to the intricate, though frequently trivial, duties of a constitutional monarch. The new King had to learn a great deal on his accession. Unfortunately for him, Lord Salisbury, his Prime Minister for the first year and a half of his reign, was on the point of retirement and apt to doze off at Cabinet meetings; he was therefore not inclined to tutor the incoming sovereign. Salisbury's successor in 1902, his nephew Arthur James Balfour, was aloof, verbally dextrous and deeply interested in philosophy and the arts. Intellectually, and in almost every other way, his tastes were diametrically opposed to those of the monarch. Henry Ponsonby, the late Queen's private secretary, had once remarked that Balfour was always 'a great success with Victoria, although to me he never seemed to treat her seriously'. He was far less of a success with King Edward, chiefly because he equally failed to treat him seriously – and this time it was noticed.

So, lacking a close and cordial relationship with his first two Prime Ministers, the King's ability to exercise a personal influence on affairs of state was correspondingly reduced. Not that Edward VII found all the activities of government interesting enough to warrant intervention: foreign policy, military and naval matters claimed his steady attention; domestic and colonial policy did not. Whereas Queen Victoria had laboured over the deskwork of a sovereign, her son was easily bored by what he considered, probably rightly, an unprofitable devotion to the minutiae of politics and diplomacy.

In one respect, however, Edward VII was scrupulous and immensely constructive. This was in introducing his heir to the mysteries of statecraft. He opened all official secrets to his son, and strove to give him confidence and insight. This was particularly necessary in two respects: one was that King Edward was determined not to repeat the unhappy history of his mother's miserly hold over official business; the other was that Prince George desperately needed much coaching and sustenance. Diffident, easily over-awed and of a conservative and rather rigid outlook, the heir to the throne benefited enormously from his father's encouragement and help.

He also benefited from the appointment of Sir Arthur Bigge as his Private Secretary. Sir Arthur held this post from 1901–31. Prince George, who frequently acknowledged the great debt he owed to his father, also readily recognised the value of Sir Arthur Bigge's advice and support, remarking that 'He taught me how to be a King.' Even before he became King, Prince George wrote to Sir Arthur, in 1907, 'I fear sometimes I have lost my temper with you and often been very rude, but I am sure you know me well enough by now to know that I did not mean it.... I am a bad hand at saying what I feel, but I thank God that I have a friend like you, in whom I have the fullest confidence and from whom I know on all occasions I shall get the best and soundest advice.'

Sir Arthur Bigge, later
Lord Stamfordham,
Private Secretary to
George v for thirty years.

The Duke of York with
New Zealand Premier
Dick Seddon at a gathering
of Maori subjects.

Soon after his father's accession to the throne, Prince George was given an ideal opportunity to extend at first hand both his knowledge of royal duties and of the British Empire. Before Queen Victoria's death it had been agreed that Prince George and Princess Mary should visit Australia to open the first Parliament of the new federation (or Commonwealth). Shortly after the Queen's funeral, the project was again discussed. King Edward, not unnaturally, did not want the Duke of York to undertake this arduous trip at such a time, and wrote that 'he had only one son left out of three and he will not have his life unnecessarily endangered for any political purpose'.

But Lord Salisbury and Arthur Balfour were convinced that the need to strengthen the bonds that existed between Britain and the colonies of white settlement was of paramount importance. Consequently Balfour wrote a clear-sighted and virtually unanswerable letter to Edward VII pointing out that

> The King is no longer merely King of Great Britain and Ireland and of a few dependencies.... He is now the greatest constitutional bond uniting together in a single Empire communities of free men separated by half the circumference of the Globe. All the patriotic sentiment which makes such an Empire possible centres in him or centres chiefly in him; and everything which emphasises his personality to our kinsmen across the seas must be a gain to the monarchy and the Empire.

King Edward gave way, and in March 1901 the Duke and Duchess of York set sail in the S.S. *Ophir*. Prince George found the double separation from his parents and from his young children hard to bear, and wrote of his departure, 'Papa proposed our healths & wished us God speed and I answered in a few words & proposed the King and Queen. I was very much affected & could hardly speak. The leave-taking was terrible. I went back with them to the yacht when I said goodbye & broke down quite.'

The voyage of the *Ophir* provided Prince George with an experience that was both maturing and illuminating. The royal party visited Gibraltar, Malta, Aden, Ceylon, Singapore, Australia, New Zealand, Mauritius, Natal, the Cape, Canada and Newfoundland. All the self-governing colonies received the Duke and Duchess of York, as did some of the naval bases

'All the patriotic sentiment which makes such an Empire possible centres in him'

and colonial possessions so essential to imperial strategy. For six months, Prince George found himself the centre of state ceremonials and diplomatic receptions, and the object of public acclamation. His self-confidence was boosted in the process, and his eyes were also opened to the astounding environmental and political variety within the self-governing portions of the Empire. Used to the patrician bearing of Lord Salisbury and Arthur Balfour, he now met Prime Ministers such as Dick Seddon of New Zealand who was homely in speech and tastes and who (according to his enemies) had never read a book in his life!

New Zealand, under the Liberal party, had developed the Empire's first Welfare State, whereas Britain did not even pay out old age pensions, let alone sickness or unemployment benefits. In some Australian states, within the new Commonwealth, Labour governments actually held office, while in Britain the Labour movement provided a puny challenge to the political domination of the Liberal and Conservative and Unionist parties. None of the self-governing colonies possessed anything like the British aristocracy. Nor was racial, ethnic or religious homogeneity to be taken for granted; in the Cape there were large numbers of Afrikaners; New Zealand had recently granted the franchise to Maori men and women; the Catholic Church was extremely strong in Australia; in Canada the French-speaking population of Quebec were by no means unanimous in their loyalty to the British throne.

The diversity and independent qualities of the steadily growing self-governing colonies impressed Prince George with some of the realities of Empire. Unlike his father, imperial developments were to remain a source of profound interest for him. Even so, the usefulness of Prince George's tour was exaggerated by contemporary opinion. Despite the evident warmth of feeling for the royal visitors, it was unthinkable that the self-governing colonies would submerge their practically independent status in some scheme of imperial federation or closer union. Growing national sentiment was incompatible with subordination to the Mother Country, though not with expressions of loyalty to the British Crown.

Prince George's view of his impact upon Australian opinion was conventional, though not without insight. Writing in 1901 to Joseph Chamberlain, the dynamic Colonial Secretary and the apostle of greater imperial unity, he observed:

> I am convinced that there exists a strong feeling of loyalty to the Crown & deep attachment to the Mother Country in Australia.... Old Colonists with whom I have talked admit that this spirit did not exist anything like to this extent, even a few years ago. They are good enough to attribute this partly to our having paid them a visit, but in my opinion the three great causes may be found in: the personal influence of & love for the Queen [Victoria], the South African War, &, if you will allow me to say so, your own indefatigable work & sympathy for this young country. Granted this happy state of things, I feel strongly that now is the time to profit by it.

Prince George's assessment of the potential of the imperial situation in 1901 was shared by many others. But the forceful initiatives of Joseph Chamberlain were generally misplaced, and doomed to failure. Organic growth was to be the hallmark of the self-governing colonies, not a prolonged Œdipus complex. Even the victorious conclusion of the South African War in May 1902 eventually proved a hollow triumph, since Afrikaner nationalism was in fact rendered even more vigorous and tenacious by that long drawn-out conflict.

Still, Prince George had done his duty, and had incidentally broadened his horizons. A week after the *Ophir* docked at Portsmouth, on 1 November 1901, King Edward created his heir Prince of Wales, and told him:

> In making you today 'Prince of Wales and Earl of Chester' I am not only conferring on you ancient titles which I have borne upwards of 59 years, but I wish to mark my appreciation of the admirable manner in which you carried out the arduous duties in the Colonies which I entrusted you with. I have but little doubts that they will bear good fruit in the future & knit the Colonies more than ever to the Mother Country.
>
> God bless you, my dear boy, & I know I can always count on your support and assistance in the heavy duties and responsible position I now occupy. Ever your devoted Papa, Edward R.I.

One of the first, and most delicate, duties that the new Prince of Wales had to undertake was a goodwill mission to Germany in January 1902, ostensibly to congratulate the Kaiser on his forty-third birthday. Goodwill was in short supply between the British and German governments. The German drive to create a High Seas Fleet could only be regarded as a serious threat to British naval supremacy. Moreover, the attempt, spearheaded by Joseph Chamberlain, to arrange an Anglo-German alliance (regarded romantically in some circles as a natural arrangement between Teuton and Anglo-Saxon) had failed.

The proposed alliance had failed chiefly because the German government had been unwilling to commit itself to the British interest without first developing the German navy, and also because of fears that there might be insufficient continuity in British foreign policy due to the electoral 'swing of the pendulum'. In the somewhat acrimonious aftermath of the negotiations for a formal alliance, Prince George's proposed visit to Berlin ran into difficulties when King Edward wrote to his nephew the Kaiser and argued that 'under the circumstances it would be better for [the Prince of Wales] not to go where he is liable to be insulted, or be treated by the public in a manner which I feel sure no one would regret more than yourself'.

Despite this frank communication, and following some diplomatic shuffling, the King was persuaded to soften his attitude, and Prince George undertook his mission. He acquitted himself well, and the Imperial German Chancellor, Prince Bulow, described him as 'clear-headed, sensible and manly'. The Kaiser's reaction was expressed in a telegram to King Edward that was redolent with family feeling: 'Georgy left this morning... all safe and sound and we were very sorry to have to part so soon from such a merry and genial guest.'

Anglo-German relations, however, were in reality no warmer after the Prince of Wales left Berlin than before. There had been no diplomatic *détente* which could be triumphantly capped by a royal visit. Fortunately this was not true of King Edward's celebrated trip to Paris in 1903. Since 1901, the British and French governments had been discussing ways of relieving tension in areas where Anglo-French interests clashed – such as Egypt, Morocco, Siam, the Newfoundland fisheries and West Africa. When King Edward subsequently visited Paris and proceeded to enchant the French with his genial *bonhomie* and evident goodwill, the foundations of the *Entente Cordiale* had been already laid.

By 1904, when the *Entente* was formalised, Britain's days of splendid isolation were doubly ended. Not only was there the new understanding with France, but since 1902 the British government had entered into a limited alliance with the newly arisen power of Japan. This alliance was extended by the Balfour government in 1905. The effect of these diplomatic initiatives was to relieve the logistical strain of maintaining imperial interests in India and the Far East alone on the one hand, and to provide Britain with a working partner in Europe on the other.

In February 1904, however, these arrangements were threatened by the outbreak of the Russo-Japanese War. Japan was Britain's ally, and France had been allied with Russia since 1894. The limited nature of the Anglo-Japanese alliance of 1902 did not require British participation in the war against Russia, but the situation was, to say the least, a delicate one. It was rendered more delicate still by the Dogger Bank Incident of October 1904, when the Russian Baltic Fleet, sailing for the eastern theatre of war, mistook some Hull trawlers for Japanese warships and opened fire on them, sinking one fishing boat and killing two of the crew.

British opinion was aghast, and a war-like clamour ensued. Prince George's reaction was run-of-the-mill and decidedly nautical: 'It seems impossible', he told his father, 'that individuals who call themselves sailors should do such a thing.... If they imagined they were Japanese destroyers, all I can say is they must have been drunk or else their nerves must be in such a state that they are not fit to go to sea in Men of War.' Happily for Britain's new understanding with France, the Russian government apologised handsomely for the disaster and paid compensation, and the Baltic fleet steamed on to be annihilated a few months later by real, not imaginary, Japanese warships. Within three years, however, the loose ends of the diplomatic confusion of 1904 were neatly tied when Britain entered into an understanding with Russia in 1907 which, though less comprehensive than the *Entente* with France, was equally beneficial.

Despite the relatively uncomplicated and quasi-ambassadorial parts he occasionally played in the diplomacy of foreign affairs, domestic and imperial policy remained of more absorbing interest to Prince George, and in October 1905 he and Princess

Edward VII's visit to Paris in 1903 symbolised the British and French Governments' desire to establish the *Entente Cordiale.*

Mary embarked on a voyage to India. The royal visit lasted six months, and took the Prince and Princess of Wales from Karachi to Mandalay, and from Lahore to Madras. As the representative of the King-Emperor, Prince George's activities were predictable enough: he shot tigers, met maharajahs, talked to British officials and to officers and men of the Indian army, officiated at reviews and durbars and, above all, allowed himself to be *seen*, as the embodiment of the imperial order.

His visit coincided with some of severest convulsions the Raj had suffered since the great Mutiny of 1857–8. The outgoing Viceroy, Lord Curzon, had resigned after a protracted and bitter quarrel with the Commander-in-Chief of the Indian Army, Lord Kitchener of Khartoum, over the control of the

military establishment. Indeed Lord Curzon's viceroyalty had been generally characterised by reforming zeal and abrasive personal contact. As almost his last act as Viceroy, he had partitioned the unwieldy and ancient province of Bengal, thus provoking an unprecendented outcry from the Bengali people and from many Indians who sympathised with them. The Indian Congress movement, for so long a harmless annual conference of landowners and intellectuals, took up the agitation.

Prince George did not believe that the Indian peoples would necessarily benefit if their representatives were admitted to a greater share in government. During his tour he talked to Gokhale, the moderate Congress leader, on the subject, telling him that he had 'been reading your speech at Benares, in which you said it would be better for India if the Indians had a much larger part in the administration. I have now been travelling for some months in India… and I have never seen a happier-looking people, and I understand the look in the eyes of the Indians. Would the peoples of India be happier if you ran the country?' Gokhale replied, 'No, Sir, I do not say they would be happier, but they would have more self-respect.'

It is doubtful if Prince George appreciated this response, and he was later to express his opposition to the India Councils Act of 1909 which granted Indians greater representation on the Central and Provincial Legislative Councils as part of the Morley-Minto reforms. His attitude towards the Raj was fundamentally similar to that of Curzon, who believed that India could be bound more closely to Britain only by the dispensation of first class and impartial administration. He had noticed, and been pained by, the way Indians were often treated by the British, and he later remarked that 'Evidently we are too much inclined to look upon them as a conquered & downtrodden race & the Native, who is becoming more and more educated, realizes this. I could not help noticing that the general bearing of the European towards the Native was to say the least unsympathetic. In fact not the same as that of superiors to inferiors at home.'

The Prince and Princess of Wales were in Burma in January 1906 when news reached them that in Britain the Liberal party had won a landslide victory in the General Election. The Balfour

78

government had resigned in December 1905 having recorded substantial success in the electorally-unstimulating fields of defence reform and foreign policy. The Liberals under Sir Henry Campbell-Bannerman had taken office, and had subsequently asked for a dissolution of Parliament. The General Election results of 1906 shattered almost twenty years of Conservative and Unionist supremacy, and gave the Liberals an overall majority of 84. Since the Liberals could, in most circumstances, count on the support of Irish Nationalist and Labour members in the House of Commons the government could reckon on 513 votes against 157, a majority of 356.

What was the full significance of this electoral revolution? Was it the triumph of the 'inferiors' over the 'superiors' that Prince George had referred to in the context of his Indian tour? Would a more intensive class war follow the dramatic increase in Labour members, who now totalled fifty-three? Prince George expressed some unease at this development, telling his father that 'I see that a great number of Labour members have been returned which is rather a dangerous sign, but I hope they are not all Socialists.'

'*I hope they are not all Socialists*'

Prince George's qualms were misplaced, for although the Liberal-Labour leader John Burns was already a member of the Cabinet, neither the government nor the House of Commons was in danger of being overrun with British Bolsheviks. Moreover Campbell-Bannerman's administration was heavy with Liberal-Imperialists, men like Asquith, Grey and Haldane, who were unlikely to dance on the ruins of Buckingham Palace.

The Liberal triumph in 1906 reflected more prosaic factors. The Balfour government of 1902–5 had held out little prospect of social reform, and it had been bitterly, and sometimes ludicrously, divided over Joseph Chamberlain's drive, from 1903, for a programme of tariff reform. The Education Act of 1902 had galvanised the Nonconformist vote against the Conservatives; accusations that indentured Chinese labourers sent to the goldfields of the Rand were, in effect, 'slaves' had stirred liberal and humanitarian consciences. All this was enough to sweep the Liberals to their last great electoral victory.

The new government faced a challenging domestic situation. The Edwardian age was troubled by internal dissension and conflict; only subsequently was it invested with the aura of a magical, never-to-be-forgotten prelude to the futility and slaughter of the Great War and to the awkward social adjustments accompanying that conflict. But the main areas of dispute and change were evident well before 1914. The war merely accelerated the pace of changes that were already under way.

Chief among the problems with which the Liberal government had to cope was that of involving the state in the support of the individual. Social welfare was anathema to many Conservatives, who argued that the aged, the poor and the unemployed had no right to state assistance, even though the Balfour government in 1905 had moved hesitantly toward certain relief measures. When in 1908 Campbell-Bannerman resigned the premiership due to failing health, and Asquith took over at No. 10 Downing Street, two significant upgradings occurred in the new Cabinet. David Lloyd George became Chancellor of the Exchequer and, in effect, paymaster of any social welfare programme, and Winston Churchill went to the Board of Trade. Churchill's patrician birth contrasted sharply with Lloyd George's commonplace Welsh origins, but both men were remarkably energetic, ambitious and able. Both practised the art of oratory with consummate skill, and lived life to the full. By 1908, moreover, both men were committed to a bold extension of social welfare; Churchill had, it seemed, just discovered the poor, but Lloyd George had known about them from birth.

Women's suffrage was another contentious issue. The Women's Social and Political Union had been founded in 1903 by Mrs Emmeline Pankhurst, supported by her daughters Christabel and Sylvia. Dubbed 'Suffragettes' by the *Daily Mail*, Mrs Pankhurst's chiefly middle-class followers began to take increasingly militant action from 1905 onwards. The response of leading statesmen to these phenomena were varied, and cut across party lines: Balfour and Campbell-Bannerman were reasonably sympathetic to the Suffragette cause, Asquith and Bonar Law were not. Moreover since more than forty per cent of Edwardian males were without the Parliamentary franchise, Lloyd George and, further to the political left, the Labour leaders argued that universal suffrage should be the object, not merely votes for women.

OPPOSITE The Coronation of Edward VII from a popular print of the time. Prince George and Princess Mary, then Duke and Duchess of York, are either side of the King and Queen Alexandra.

LEFT Slum children in 1910.

RIGHT Two aspiring Liberal Ministers, Lloyd George and Winston Churchill, who though from vastly different backgrounds were committed to social reform.

To the controversy over women's suffrage was added the more menacing problem of industrial conflict. Between 1901 and 1913 trade union membership increased from a little over 2,000,000 to more than 4,100,000. The poor housing conditions in many of Britain's great cities, the lack of real educational opportunity, long hours of work and uncertain rates of pay, were all part of the sharp contrast between the standard of living of working-class and middle-class families. Yet, until 1911, trades union activity was strangely muted. This was partly due to the hope that the Liberal government would legislate to benefit the working man, and partly because Labour representatives in the House of Commons realised that their spectacular success in the election of 1906 had been made possible largely by an electoral pact with the Liberals. Still, these restraints were not likely to prove permanent.

Nor was the comparatively quiescent state of Ireland. The Gladstonian initiatives to solve the Irish problem had foundered with the Home Rule Bills of 1886 and 1893. After 1906 the

Both George v and his son Albert (later George vi) were second sons and so destined for a naval career. In 1891 Prince George commanded the gunboat HMS *Thrush*, shown on the right of Edward de Martino's picture of The Channel Squadron, 1898 (above). Prince Albert served in the Royal Navy during the Great War and was a Sub-Lieutenant on HMS *Collingwood* at the battle of Jutland. BELOW A painting of the battle by Robert H. Smith.

Liberals tried to allay Irish grievances piecemeal, by ending coercion and improving conditions of tenantry, housing and education. An Irish Councils Bill was introduced in 1907, but its provisions for local government reorganisation were unlikely to satisfy Irish nationalist demands. While the Liberals possessed an overall majority in the House of Commons, they had no need to bow to Irish pressure and risk electoral unpopularity. But in 1909 Lloyd George's first budget began a sequence of events which produced one of the gravest domestic crises in recent British history, and promoted a threatening coalescence of many of the more uncomfortable pressures upon Edwardian society.

Lloyd George's 'People's Budget' of 1909 was not necessarily designed to be rejected by the House of Lords. Since 1906 the Lords had certainly obstructed important pieces of Liberal legislation, including Birrell's Education Bill, the Plural Voting Bill and the Land Valuation Bill. A head-on collision between the elected Lower House and the hereditary, and overwhelmingly Conservative, Upper House seemed increasingly likely. The 1909 budget, however, brought matters to a climax. The Chancellor needed to find nearly £16,000,000 to pay for the old-age pensions scheme and for the recently extended building programme for the Royal Navy. He decided to soak the rich, and the budget raised the rate of tax on all unearned incomes and on earned incomes that exceeded £3,000 per annum. A super-tax was levied on incomes of more than £5,000, and increased death, tobacco and spirit duties imposed. Most provocative of all was the introduction of a new revenue tax on land, which was a blow not only against the Lords, but against landlords in general.

The Conservatives, convinced that confiscatory socialism was about to grip the land, prepared to reject the budget in the House of Lords. They denounced Lloyd George for waging a war on property, while the Chancellor declared that he was in fact leading a crusade against poverty and squalor. In November 1909, the Lords vetoed the budget by 350 votes to 75, thus violating the constitutional convention that the Upper House should not tamper with the annual Finance Bill. The Prime Minister, Asquith, called for dissolution of Parliament and a General Election. After a bitterly-fought campaign, and a

THE NEW YEAR'S GIFT.

bumper turn-out of voters (86.6 per cent), the Liberals were returned to power in January 1910. Their overall majority, however, had vanished and they found themselves dependent upon Irish and Labour support in the Commons.

The King's Speech which opened the New Parliament contained the announcement that the constitutional powers of the House of Lords would be amended. In April 1910, Asquith presented the Parliament Bill to the Commons, making clear that if the Lords rejected this measure he would again appeal to the country and seek the King's guarantee that, if necessary, he would create sufficient Liberal peers to out-vote the Conservatives in the Upper House. Within a few days the Lords passed the People's Budget, and instead concentrated their attention upon the Parliament Bill.

Before the final blows could be struck, however, King Edward died. On 4 May, Prince George had noted 'went over

OPPOSITE A *Punch* cartoon from January 1909 comments on a belated reform.

BELOW A still youthful Queen Alexandra pays a last tribute to her dying husband as portrayed in a contemporary illustration.

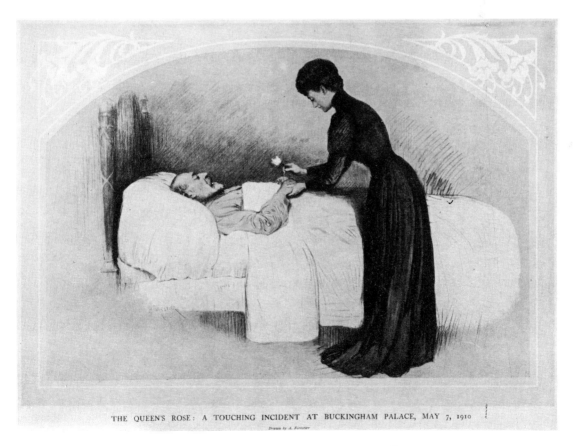

THE QUEEN'S ROSE: A TOUCHING INCIDENT AT BUCKINGHAM PALACE, MAY 7, 1910

Drawn by A. Forestier

to B.P. [Buckingham Palace] & saw Papa; his colour was bad and his breathing fast'. The King was suffering from a serious attack of bronchitis and his condition was about to deteriorate sharply. On 6 May, he smoked a large cigar at noon and ate a light lunch, but then suffered a series of heart attacks. As the King's life slipped away, the Prince of Wales was able to tell him that his horse *Witch of the Air* had won that afternoon at Kempton Park. It was, appropriately enough, virtually the last news that he heard. At 11.45 in the evening he died, and the nation mourned a sovereign who by his gusto, charm and dignity had done much to increase the popularity of the monarchy.

The new King recorded in his diary: 'I have lost my best friend and the best of fathers. I never had a word with him in his life. I am heartbroken & overwhelmed with grief, but God will help me in my great responsibilities & darling May will be my comfort as she always has been.' With party warfare over the Parliament Bill merely suspended, and with Ireland, trades union militancy and the German naval threat to contain, the early years of King George v's reign promised to be turbulent ones.

OPPOSITE Lightning crackles round Westminster Hall as crowds queue to file past the body of Edward VII.

4 King Amid Crisis 1910-14

PRINCE GEORGE ascended the throne as Halley's comet blazed in the night skies. A more superstitious age would have attempted to interpret this phenomenon appropriately, but in London the trumpets merely rang out to proclaim a new sovereign, 'George the Fifth by the Grace of God, King of the United Kingdom of Great Britain and Ireland, and of the British Dominions beyond the Seas, Defender of the Faith, Emperor of India'. A week later, the body of King Edward was buried at Windsor at a service attended by the royal family and a galaxy of foreign dignitaries that included the Kaiser, the Kings of Denmark, Portugal, Spain, Norway, Belgium, Greece and Bulgaria, the Dowager Empress of Russia, the Archduke Franz Ferdinand of Austria, assorted Crown Princes and ex-President Theodore Roosevelt of the United States.

A year later King George and Queen Mary were crowned amid gorgeous ceremonial and great popular acclaim. If foreign potentates had been much in evidence at King Edward's funeral, the coronation of George v saw a massive joint tribute by the members of the British Empire. There were now four Dominions to be represented, since the proclamation of the Union of South Africa in 1910. In the coronation procession marched troops from the Indian Empire, from West and East Africa, from Ceylon and Malaya, from the West Indies and the East Indies, and from many other portions of the Empire. The hereditary 'King's champion' bore the standard of England, the Duke of Wellington carried the Union Flag and two of Britain's most distinguished soldiers, Lord Roberts and Lord Kitchener, carried the swords of spiritual and temporal justice respectively.

King George's own account of his coronation day is both matter-of-fact and moving – a naval log book spattered with tears:

It was overcast & cloudy with some showers & a strongish cool breeze, but better for the people than great heat. Today was indeed a great & memorable day in our lives & one we can never forget, but it brought back to me many sad memories of 9 years ago, when the beloved Parents were crowned. May & I left B.P. in the Coronation coach at 10.30 with 8 cream coloured horses. There were over 50,000 troops lining the streets under the command of Lord Kitchener. There were hundreds of thousands of people who

PREVIOUS PAGES
The transport strikers march across Tower Bridge on their way to Southwark Park in July 1912.

OPPOSITE Part of the Coronation of George v by Bacon.

gave us a magnificent reception. The service in the Abbey was most beautiful, but it was a terrible ordeal. It was grand, yet simple & most dignified and went without a hitch. I nearly broke down when dear David came to do homage to me, as it reminded me so much when I did the same thing to beloved Papa.... Worked all the afternoon with Bigge & others answering telegrams and letters of which I have had hundreds.... Our guests dined with us at 8.30. May & I showed ourselves again to the people. Wrote & read. Rather tired. Bed at 11.45. Beautiful illuminations everywhere.

The ancient traditions of the coronation ceremony underwent one significant innovation, when the King's coronation oath was shorn of a paragraph that could be offensive to Catholics. Instead, the sovereign undertook simply to maintain the Protestant religion and the Protestant succession. The Irish subjects of King George were the main beneficiaries of this exercise in tact, but the Welsh people were also accorded a handsome gesture when, in July 1911, three weeks after the coronation, the King's eldest son was presented as Prince of Wales to the Welsh nation at a ceremony at Caernarvon Castle. The details of the investiture were more the result of inspiration and a sense of the theatrical than anything else. After all, it was more than six hundred years since Edward I had presented his son to the Welsh as their prince; there were no precedents to go on. But David Lloyd George, the master of improvisation, put his talents to work and even taught the Prince to say in Welsh 'All Wales is a sea of song' and 'Thanks from the bottom of my heart to the old land of my fathers.' These bilingual forrays, though not altogether appropriate, were rapturously received.

Behind the scenes, however, the preparation for the investiture ceremony had been stormy. Queen Mary recorded that, on the day, 'David looked charming in his purple and miniver cloak & gold circlet & did his part very well. The heat was awful.' But Prince Edward was later to recall how much he had disliked his fancy costume and dreaded to think what his fellow naval cadets at Dartmouth would make of it. In his memoirs as Duke of Windsor he wrote, 'There was a family blow-up that night, but in the end my mother, as always, smoothed things over.' Queen Mary apparently sorted out the problem by telling her son not to take the ceremony too seriously, and assuring him that his friends would realise that, as

OPPOSITE King George presents the Prince of Wales to the people at the investiture in Caernarvon Castle. The Prince was greatly embarrassed by his fancy costume but Queen Mary thought he 'looked charming'.

ABOVE the front and back
of a coronation mug.

LEFT a goblet made for
the coronation in 1911.

prince, he was obliged to do some things that might appear a little silly.

The 'family blow-up' that preceded the investiture at Caernarvon was indicative of growing tensions between King George and Queen Mary on the one hand, and their children on the other. King George was devoted to his family, yet he found it difficult to develop, especially with his growing sons, the sort of rapport that had existed between himself and his own father. Monogamous, unsophisticated, direct and meticulous, he has been described as a martinet when it came to family discipline. The Duke of Windsor later recalled that 'The laws of behaviour as revealed to a small boy tended to be ruled by a vast preponderance of "don'ts". But with Mama life was less severe. Although she backed up my father in all matters of discipline, she never failed to take our side whenever in her judgment he was being too harsh with us.'

Queen Mary had her blind spots too. She took no great joy in the process of pregnancy and childbirth, and subsequently left a great deal of baby-care to royal nurses and nannies. Both she and King George were unduly perturbed by childish idiosyncracies, as when she wrote that her eldest son David 'was "jumpy" yesterday morning, however he got quieter after being out, what a curious child he is'. Moreover, it took the royal couple three years to realise that Prince Edward's first nurse (perhaps wishing to have the baby more to herself) frequently pinched him before presenting him to his parents with the result that the crying child was soon handed back to her. Not surprisingly, this nurse eventually suffered a nervous breakdown, and it was revealed that she had not taken a day's holiday for the last three years!

The royal children had also suffered from early and pro-longed separations from their parents. When Duchess of York, Princess Mary had found on her return from the seven and a half months' voyage of the *Ophir* in 1901 that 'the younger children had grown and altered so much that when I got back, they seemed like little strangers'. In October 1905, Prince George and Princess Mary had embarked on their six months' tour of the Indian Empire. During both these absences the children's royal and zestful grandparents had, allegedly, spoiled and indulged them. Queen Alexandra, for instance, had insisted on bathing them at whatever time she chose, and had also connived at indiscipline by pretending to drink from glasses that her grandsons had filled liberally with pepper and salt.

On George V's accession, Prince Edward was nearly sixteen years old, Prince Albert was fourteen, Princess Mary twelve, Prince Henry ten, Prince George eight and Prince John five. The three eldest children were thus in the throes of adolescence when their demanding and sometimes irascible father took up the weighty responsibilities of kingship. Given their parents somewhat unyielding concept of what constituted good behaviour, and the not inconsiderable disadvantages of royal birth, it is perhaps not surprising that Prince Edward soon showed signs of a restlessness almost equivalent to that of his grandfather King Edward, or that Prince Albert became the victim of a speech impediment that remained with him throughout life.

King George also faced problems of a more public nature in 1910. Asquith, the Prime Minister, did not wish immediately to embroil the new King in the Parliament Bill controversy. He later recalled that his reaction, on hearing of King Edward's death, was to realise that George V, 'with all his fine and engaging qualities, was without political experience. We were nearing the verge of a crisis almost without example in our constitutional history. What was the right thing to do?'

After a meeting with the monarch, which he left 'deeply moved by the King's modesty and good sense', Asquith arranged an interparty conference with the agreement of Balfour, the Leader of the Opposition. This at least gave King George a six months' reprieve from the awkward questions raised by the constitutional crisis. It incidentally gave Asquith a reprieve from Irish nationalist pressure for action on the Home Rule issue. Irish Nationalist MPs had found themselves holding the balance in the Commons, together with Labour members, after the General Election results of January 1910 had left the Liberals with a majority of only two over the Conservatives.

By November 1910, the interparty constitutional conference had foundered over Home Rule. Asquith, with the Cabinet's approval, then asked the King for a dissolution of Parliament. Eventually the Prime Minister extracted from the King a secret undertaking that if the forthcoming general election kept

OPPOSITE A photo taken at Abergeldie of the Royal Family in 1906. The baby Prince John suffered from epilepsy and died while still a child. The other children from left to right are Princess Mary, later the Princess Royal, Prince George (Duke of Kent), Prince Henry (Duke of Gloucester), Prince Edward (Edward VIII) and Prince Albert (George VI).

the government in power then, if necessary, up to five hundred Liberal peers would be created to enable the Parliament Bill to be placed on the statute books. George V was reluctant to give this undertaking, and particularly despondent that it should be a secret one. He told Lord Esher 'I have never in my life done anything I was ashamed to confess. And I have never been accustomed to conceal things.'

The General Election of December 1910 provided a dead-heat between the two major parties, and Asquith continued to hold office on the sufferance of non-Liberal votes in the Commons. After much heart-searching within the Conservative and Unionist ranks, the House of Lords passed the Parliament Bill in August 1911. With the King's secret assurance to Asquith now revealed, the bulk of Conservative peers (the 'hedgers') abstained, though 114 (the 'ditchers') did indeed go to the last ditch and voted against the Bill.

Ironically it was the votes of thirty-seven Conservative peers, led by Lord Curzon, that got the Bill through by a majority of seventeen, thus avoiding the 'pollution' of the peerage by potential Liberal lords like Thomas Hardy, J. M. Barrie and Bertrand Russell. King George was greatly relieved, and wrote, 'I am afraid it is impossible to pat the Opposition on the back, but I am indeed grateful for what they have done & saved me from a humiliation which I should never have survived. If the creation had taken place, I should never have been the same person again.'

Within three months of the passing of the Parliament Bill, the King and Queen left to hold a Coronation Durbar at Delhi. King George had put this proposal to Asquith in the autumn of 1910, and soon afterwards wrote to Lord Morley, the Secretary of State for India, arguing:

> Ever since I visited India five years ago I have been impressed by the great advantage which would result from a visit by the sovereign to that great Empire. The events which have unfortunately occurred since 1906 have only strengthened that opinion. I am convinced that if it were possible for me, accompanied by the Queen, to ... hold a Coronation Durbar at Delhi, where we should meet all the Princes, officials and vast numbers of the People, the greatest benefits would accrue to the Country at large. I also trust and I believe, that if the proposed visit could be made known some

time before, it would tend to allay unrest and, I am sorry to say, seditious spirit, which unfortunately exists in some parts of India.

The Cabinet eventually agreed to the royal visit, but with some misgivings over the huge expenses that would be incurred by the government of India. Some of the details of the Durbar ceremony also proved troublesome. It was finally decided, for example, that the King-Emperor would not crown himself (thus invoking unwelcome comparisons with Napoleon Bonaparte), nor be crowned by an Anglican bishop before a multitude of Hindus, Muslims and Sikhs; instead he would appear with his crown already on! But which crown? There were legal difficulties over removing the royal regalia from Britain, so a special crown had to be made for the occasion. There was nothing lightweight about this splendid piece of headgear, and King George later wrote 'Rather tired after wearing the Crown for $3\frac{1}{2}$ hours, it hurt my head, as it is pretty heavy.'

Then there was the problem of the King-Emperor's entry into Delhi through the ancient gate once used by the Mogul Emperors. An elephant was the appropriate mount for an Emperor of India, but the plans were for a procession headed by high officials on horseback. When King George at last entered Delhi on horseback wearing a field marshal's uniform and topee, and flanked by British officials, the Indian crowds apparently failed to recognise him and his reception was a chilly one.

Tigers provided as much trouble as elephants and horses in planning the royal visit, but this time because the King wanted to fit a week's tiger-shooting into his already heavy itinerary. George v was an expert marksman, and rifle-shooting, together with stamp-collecting and sailing, was a keenly pursued hobby. 'The fact is', wrote the new Secretary of State for India, Lord Crewe, 'that it is a misfortune for a public personage to have any taste so strongly developed as the craze for shooting is in our beloved Ruler.' But royal persistence prevailed, and King George went off to bag his tigers while Queen Mary, who had read a number of serious books to prepare her for her Indian tour, visited Agra and the Taj Mahal.

The Durbar took place on 12 December 1911. The Viceroy, Lord Hardinge, led the Indian princes in an hour long ceremony

of homage to the King-Emperor, whose train was carried by six pages who were either maharajahs or the sons of maharajahs. Fifty thousand troops paraded before the royal couple, and the massed bands numbered more than one and a half thousand men. The climax of the ceremony came when King George announced two major boons to the people of India: one was the ending of Lord Curzon's unpopular partition of Bengal in 1905; the second was the transference of British India's capital from Calcutta to refurbished New Delhi. Neither of these boons was particularly useful in upholding the Raj. Since many Indian nationalists found the Morley-Minto reforms of 1909 inadequate, the reunification of Bengal could not begin to buy off agitation against British rule. Moreover, the transference of the capital to Delhi had ominous significance in Indian tradition, which held that the collapse of the ruling power invariably followed such a move.

The overall effect of the King and Queen's visit to India can be diversely interpreted. For King George, who took his ceremonial functions so earnestly, the Durbar perfectly symbolised his lonely, exalted and semi-divine status as King-Emperor. His confidence was increased, but so perhaps was his sense of isolation. However, he noted with pleasure that after the restrained reception he had received at Delhi, the tour had gathered momentum, until in potentially seditious Calcutta 'the people became more & more enthusiastic each day & were quite as demonstrative as they are in England, which is most unusual in the Indian people.'

Viewed more dispassionately, the impact of King George's Durbar on the course of Indian history was hardly profound. The crowds milling in the streets did not control the Congress movement. Nor was the King justified in putting so much trust in the support of the Indian princes, who ruled nearly a third of the sub-continent. Nationalist leaders did not want to exchange the incorruptible paternalism of the Indian Civil Service for the erratic paternalism of the Indian aristocracy. Indeed, if the Raj was ever dismantled then the independent power of the maharajahs would, in all probability, be destroyed at the same time. Such speculation, however, would have seemed inappropriate to the King-Emperor and to the vast majority of the British community in India in 1911. Few expected the Raj to

OPPOSITE Unfortunately the crowd did not recognise the King among the many personalities riding through the Mogul Gate into Delhi and his reception was cool.

The Coronation Durbar at Delhi

The Durbar was the King's idea as his earlier visits to India had convinced him that a royal trip would bring 'greatest benefits' to the country and 'tend to allay unrest'. After a cool reception the enthusiasm of the Indian people increased greatly during the tour and became in the King's words 'as demonstrative as in England'.

BELOW The King on a tiger hunt (on the centre elephant).

LEFT The King and Queen at Calcutta preparing to leave India.

BELOW An ornate parasol shields the Queen from the Indian sun.

come tumbling down within the next thirty-six years. The Delhi Durbar was, however, both the ceremonial apotheosis of the Indian Empire and a rare, isolated moment stolen from the pressures of nationalist agitation.

When King George and Queen Mary returned to Britain in February 1912, they found that domestic industrial unrest was about to express itself in a national coal strike. Trade union militancy had increased sharply after 1910, when unemployment reached its lowest point since the turn of the century, thus reducing the supply of blackleg labour available to employers. The rising cost of living (fourteen per cent during the seven years preceeding 1913) and the apparent ineffectualness of Labour representatives in the Commons strengthened the unions' appeal to the workers. The uncertain legal status of trades unions had been underlined by the 1905 Osborne judgment which had ruled that it was illegal for unions to collect funds from their members for political purposes. This had struck a serious blow at the financing of the Labour party, and even when the 1913 Trade Union Act restored the power of political levy, it also allowed individual union members to opt out of such schemes.

Disillusionment with the Liberal government and with Labour MPs encouraged syndicalists and others to argue that direct industrial action, and even workers' control, were essential in bringing capitalism down. During 1911 one strike had followed another as the seamen, the dockers, the railwaymen and other, smaller, unions had stopped work. The coal strike that greeted King George on his return from India was ended only after six weeks, when the government intervened and established district boards to fix wages. In the summer of 1912, London dockers and lightermen also struck. By the end of the year nearly forty-one million working days had been lost due to strikes. A measure like Lloyd George's National Insurance Act of 1911 watered down working-class grievances, but it could not possibly by itself eliminate discontent.

The King was disturbed by the clangour of class conflict that frequently manifested itself during these bitter industrial disputes. There was even talk of revolution, and during the rail strike of August 1911 the Aldershot garrison was transferred to London, special constables were enrolled and gunsmiths did a handsome trade. But Swindon did not become a syndicalist citadel, nor did the red flag fly over St Pancras station. J.H. Thomas, the railwaymen's leader, was persuaded by Lloyd George to call off the strikes after only three days. The King then wrote to the Chancellor of the Exchequer saying 'I heartily congratulate you and feel that the whole country will be most grateful to you for averting a most disastrous calamity. It has caused me the greatest possible anxiety.'

King George and Queen Mary, although deploring un-employment and giving money privately to allay its effects, seem to have viewed strike action chiefly as an unfortunate dis-ruption of national activity. When a strike of transport workers followed the 1912 railway stoppage Queen Mary wrote, 'Now we have a transport strike which may become very serious – really we have no luck, one tiresome thing after another.'

A more perceptive onlooker might have seen that it was the working man who had recently had no luck; between 1900 and 1911 the purchasing power of the pound had dropped by twenty-five per cent while the average weekly wage had risen by a mere 2¼d. Since government intervention in industrial disputes was an innovation, regarded with much suspicion by those who preferred to put their trust in the free play of economic forces, the unions simply could not rely on minis-terial initiatives to help solve their members' justifiable griev-ances. Nor did King George's periodic visits to industrialised areas provide any improvement in the material wellbeing of his poorer subjects. It was thus understandable that during 1913–14 the union leaders of the miners, railwaymen and dockers dis-cussed a common approach to their problems. The Great War diverted the unions' energies from such schemes, but this was to prove only a respite.

Suffragette militancy also increased between 1910 and 1914. In 1913, the government-sponsored Franchise and Registration Bill carried an amendment which would have extended the franchise to women house-holders over twenty-five years of age. The Speaker, however, ruled that the Bill was technically unacceptable due to its amended nature. The Suffragettes, who had long since graduated from heckling public figures to window-smashing and arson, stepped up their agitation. Mrs Pankhurst was sentenced to three years' imprisonment after a

'Really we have no luck, one tiresome thing after another'

A scene of distress in
the East End in 1912.

bomb exploded in a house being constructed for Lloyd George. There were physical assaults on other Cabinet ministers, and during the 1913 Derby Emily Davidson threw herself under the King's horse and sustained fatal injuries. King George and Queen Mary both detested disorder, and the violent public manifestations of Suffragette feeling upset and antagonised them. On witnessing Emily Davidson's suicidal act, Queen Mary's first thought was for the jockey 'poor Jones... who was much knocked about'. As for the unfortunate Miss Davidson, the Queen wrote (before she knew the full extent of the disaster) 'the horrid woman was injured but not seriously'.

Although the King also felt little sympathy for Mrs Pankhurst's followers, he was concerned at the methods of forcible feeding used with imprisoned Suffragettes who were on hunger strikes. Early in 1913, he let the Home Secretary, Reginald McKenna, know that 'His Majesty cannot help feeling that there is something shocking, if not almost cruel, in the operation to which these insensate women are subjected.... His Majesty concludes that Miss Pankhurst's description of what she endured when forcibly fed is more or less true. If so, her story will horrify people otherwise not in sympathy with the Militant Suffragettes.' In fact, the excesses of the Suffragette extremists alienated many potential sympathisers during the years 1913–14, even provoking the *Manchester Guardian* to decry 'diseased emotionalism'. The outbreak of war in August 1914 brought a halt in the agitation when Mrs Pankhurst and her supporters patriotically curtailed their campaign.

The government attempted to put an even more contentious issue into cold storage when the war began. This was the Irish Home Rule Bill. Since 1910, the Asquith government had been dependant on Irish nationalist support in the Commons. Pressured by J. E. Redmond, leader of the Irish Nationalist MPs, the government introduced a Home Rule Bill in April 1912. The chief clauses of the Bill were mild enough, simply providing for an Irish Parliament in Dublin, consisting of two chambers, and able to legislate on all Irish matters not reserved for the Imperial Parliament at Westminster. These reserved items were such that even if the Bill had been passed at once, the Irish would have been left with a sadly emasculated independence. But the Bill did not, of course, pass the Conservative and

Unionist-dominated House of Lords. The peers threw it out in 1912, and again in 1913. The Parliament Act of 1911, however, now limited the delaying powers of the Upper House to two years, and by 1914 the Bill merely awaited the royal assent. Ancient hostilities and passionate convictions had been aroused during these two years.

Fundamentally, the controversy centred on the refusal of the Protestant majority in Ulster to accept rule by the Catholic south. In 1886, Lord Randolph Churchill had rashly proclaimed during the first Home Rule crisis that 'Ulster will fight and Ulster will be right.' By 1914, Ulster was, indeed, prepared to fight; led by Sir Edward Carson, the barrister who had prosecuted Oscar Wilde, nearly a quarter of a million men had signed the belligerent Ulster Covenant; the Ulster Volunteers were formed and arms were landed from Germany. In Britain, public figures like Rudyard Kipling, Field Marshal Lord Roberts of Kandahar and Edward Elgar supported the cause of Ulster.

ABOVE LEFT Miss Sylvia Pankhurst painting the shopfront of the Women's Social Defence League in Bow Road.

ABOVE The funeral
procession of Emily
Davidson who threw
herself under the King's
horse at the Derby in 1913.

HOME CHAT: A STUDY IN DOMESTICITY.

Mr. Asquith. "PRESENTING, AS THEY DO, A SOLID AND UNITED FRONT, WE PROPOSE TO HAND OVER TO THE IRISH THE ABSOLUTE CONTROL OF THEIR DOMESTIC AFFAIRS."

So, inevitably, did the Conservative and Unionist opposition, now led by the hard-hitting Bonar Law who had replaced the urbane and academic Balfour in 1911. Bonar Law, though prepared in the last resort to compromise with the government over Home Rule, used a variety of techniques to discomfort the Liberals. One technique was to try to convince King George that he should withhold the royal assent to the Home Rule Bill. In 1912, Bonar Law, according to Austen Chamberlain's account, told the King that unless the government resigned within the next two years 'you must either accept the Home Rule Bill or dismiss your Ministers and choose others who will support you in vetoing it: and in either case, half your subjects will think you have acted against them'. The King apparently 'turned red at this', and admitted that he had never considered these possibilities. Law then said 'They may say that your Assent is a purely formal act and the prerogative of veto is dead. That was true as long as there was a buffer between you and the House of Commons, but they have destroyed this buffer [the House of Lords before the Parliament Act reforms] and it is true no longer.'

Bonar Law was probably right in claiming that this conversation gave King George the worst five minutes he had experienced for a long time. But other public and private pressures were soon to be put upon the sovereign. Among the latter were the anonymous letters that flooded into Buckingham Palace, some abusing the King, others begging him not to hand over loyal Ulster to the Pope and the College of Cardinals! By August 1913, King George was convinced that he was being placed in an impossible constitutional position and that therefore he should put a compromise proposal to the Prime Minister. The King had a warm personal regard for Asquith, whom he distinctly preferred to Bonar Law, nonetheless he had grown impatient with the policy of 'wait and see'. The Prime Minister had relied on this enigmatic formula as the Parliament Bill crisis deepened; he now seemed content with a similar attitude towards Home Rule.

In August 1913, the King, therefore, sent a detailed memorandum to Asquith saying, among other things, that he felt that no other sovereign had ever been in so delicate a constitutional position, and that he could not 'help feeling that the Govern-

OPPOSITE A *Punch* cartoon caricatures Asquith's proposals to solve the Irish Question.

OVERLEAF
The Delhi Durbar by Jacomb-Hood.

113

King George with his cousins the Kaiser (far picture) and the Tsar (right) in 1913. Their close family connections could not prevent war breaking out a year later. Of the three cousins only George, the · constitutional monarch, survived the Great War with life and throne intact.

ment is drifting and taking me with it'. He proposed a con-ference to settle the problem, and mentioned a possible arrangement whereby Ulster could contract out of the Home Rule scheme. These sensible suggestions were later reiterated in a lengthy letter which the King sent to his Prime Minister.

Perhaps chiefly because the government wanted a peaceful settlement of the Home Rule issue, the King's proposals, which were not unique in themselves, were eventually acted upon. When Asquith introduced the second reading of the Home Rule Bill in March 1914, he offered Ulster the right to opt out for six years. Sir Edward Carson defiantly rejected this suggestion, saying 'We do not want a sentence of death with a stay of execution for six years.'

Ten days later, fifty-eight senior and junior army officers at the Curragh camp near Dublin informed Sir Arthur Paget, the commander of British forces in Ireland, that they would resign their commissions rather than agree to take part in active operations in Ulster. The British government later denied that any ultimatum had been sent via General Paget, and the embarrassment engendered by this gentlemanly army mutiny in Ireland abated. It was an ominous sign, however, that civil war could indeed break out over Ulster.

On 21 July 1914, the King opened a conference on the Home Rule issue attended by two representatives of the government, the opposition, the Ulster loyalists and the Irish Nationalists. The conference failed, though both sides were now prepared to compromise over the exclusion of Ulster. The breaking-point came with an attempt to define Ulster geographically, and particularly in deciding the fate of counties Tyrone and Fermanagh, which were both almost equally divided between Protestants and Catholics. The King was convinced that the conference had, nevertheless, created a 'more friendly understanding'. To others it seemed that Ireland might yet become the theatre for civil war and that new and bloodier battles might well be fought on the banks of the Boyne.

As it happened, the battle lines of an infinitely greater conflict were being drawn up as the conference on Ireland ended. Ministers who had been wrestling with the complex but parochial problems of Tyrone and Fermanagh were startled to receive, on 24 July 1914, the text of an ultimatum from the Austro-Hungarian government to Serbia. Almost a month had passed since the Austrian Archduke Franz Ferdinand had been assassinated in the Bosnian capital of Sarajevo by Serbian nationalists. Now the Austro-Hungarian ultimatum contained demands which could not possibly be met by Serbia; Russia as the champion of the Slav people would be obliged to move against Austria; Germany would support her Austrian ally; France could not allow German mobilisation to proceed unanswered; Britain had entered into an intimate understanding with France.

The logistics of war, the detailed plans of the European high commands, the essential time-tabling of mobilisation and troop movements, pushed Austria, Germany, Russia and France towards a conflict which all governments had hoped to avoid. For a few days, Britain stood aloof while European heads of state and governments bombarded each other with proposals and counter-proposals designed to halt the march to war. Finally, Britain, after provoking French fears that she might remain neutral, sent an ultimatum to Germany, demanding an end to the violation of neutral Belgian territory. The ultimatum expired on 4 August. The previous day Sir Edward Grey, ornithologist, fisherman and Foreign Secretary since 1905, had reminded the House of Commons of Britain's obligations to France and Belgium, and, anticipating a short conflict, said 'If we are engaged in war we shall suffer but little more than if we stand aside.'

Prince Albert, known to the family as Bertie, in the Royal Navy in 1914.

King George, whose second son was with the Royal Navy, expressed feelings which were both more commonplace and more human:

Tuesday August 4th. I held a Council at 10.45 to declare war with Germany. It is a terrible catastrophe, but it is not our fault. An enormous crowd collected outside the Palace; we went on the balcony both before and after dinner. When they heard that war had been declared, the excitement increased & May & I with David went on to the balcony; the cheering was terrific. Please God it may soon be over & that he will protect dear Bertie's life.

ountry 1914-18

As the British government's ultimatum to Germany expired on the evening of 4 August 1914, the Foreign Secretary Sir Edward Grey watched the gas lights being dimmed in Whitehall and said 'The lights are going out all over Europe. We shall not see them lit again in our lifetime.' This gloomily enigmatic remark from a somewhat gloomy and enigmatic man was subsequently suffused with the value of a weighty valediction, even with the gift of prescience.

In a sense, Grey was wrong on both counts. Europe did indeed emerge much altered from the trauma of the Great War: crowned heads had toppled, the Bolsheviks had arisen; the 'flappers' were on the way in, nannies and parlour-maids were on the way out; the needs of the state had tempered the freedom of the individual, the new freedoms of the individual had altered the structure of many states. Yet the pre-war period had been one of great upheaval and conflict, and in 1911 Winston Churchill had said 'all the world is changing at once'. There was, therefore, no era of placid and universal contentment to be shattered in 1914.

Nor were the lights of European civilisation, attainment and culture dimmed for a lifetime. By the time Grey himself died in 1933, a new and dazzling array had long been lit: the League of Nations provided a unique forum for international discussion; whole nations had been given their independence at the end of the war; the spread of literacy, the revolutions in design, art and literature, the new means of mass communication, contained infinite promise for mankind, as well as, in the case of broadcasting and the talking films, some ominous potential as propaganda media.

The outbreak of war was attended by much public hysteria and a display of official phlegm. As in Berlin, St Petersburg, Vienna and Paris, in London the crowds exulted in the declaration of hostilities. The well-springs of patriotism had been tapped, but so too had the unthinking jingoism which had attended, for example, the Battle of Omdurman and the relief of Mafeking. For many, the coming war ended, at least for the moment, the uncertainties of the Edwardian situation when, in the words of the Liberal journalist and politician C.F.G. Masterman, written in 1909, 'We can find no answer to the inquiry, whether we are about to plunge into a new period of

PREVIOUS PAGES A file of East Yorks picking their way round shell craters in Fregenburg.

ABOVE Jubilant
London crowds
cheer the
declaration of war.

Four million Tipperary kerchiefs were sold during the war.

tumult and upheaval, whether we are destined to an indefinite prolongation of the present half-lights and shadows, whether, as we sometimes try to anticipate, a door is about to be opened, revealing unimaginable glories.'

Asquith and the administration approached matters more pragmatically. With the exception of Winston Churchill at the Admiralty, Cabinet members did not rejoice at the scent of battle, and Lord Morley, indeed, resigned. The Prime Minister understood little of military matters and proposed to let the generals and admirals run the war while the government carried on more or less as usual. After all, Britain's strategic role seemed quite straightforward: the Royal Navy would meet the German High Seas fleet and destroy it; a British Expeditionary

Force would be sent to France to plug a gap or two, while French forces in the west and the Russian 'steamroller' in the east pounded the German and Austrian armies into submission. It was confidently expected in many circles that the war would be over by Christmas, and that civilian life would have hardly been disturbed in the process.

At first, this prognosis seemed correct. To the strains of *It's a Long Way to Tipperary* the small British Expeditionary Force crossed the Channel and marched to Mauberge in northern France; the Russian armies poured into East Prussia; the Royal Navy belligerently rode the waves. Then everything began to go wrong for the Allies. The Germans routed the Russians at Tannenberg and again at the battle of the Masurian Lakes in East Prussia and, further south, successfully propped up the Austrian forces in Galicia. The advance of the German armies through Belgium and northern France was halted only with difficulty at the battles of the Marne and First Ypres. By November 1914, both sides had fought themselves to a standstill in the west, and had dug in behind a line of trenches that ran from the Swiss frontier to the sea. The horrors of trench warfare were a poor exchange for the dashing campaigns of great armies that everyone had expected. Even at sea there were unexpected setbacks, when on 22 September one German U-boat sank three British battlecruisers, and when, a month later, another U-boat penetrated the defences of the great naval base at Scapa Flow and sank the battleship *Audacious*.

It was evident towards the end of 1914 that, far from being over by Christmas, the war would require a colossal and unprecedented outpouring of men, money and munitions from the British people. Lord Kitchener, the conqueror of Dervishes and Boers, had taken over the War Office soon after hostilities began; he immediately began to conjure up a huge new volunteer army to replace the veterans of the BEF which was soon to be shattered at Mons and Ypres; in all, more than two and a half million men had volunteered by the time conscription was introduced in March 1916.

Naval organisation, however, was the subject of fierce controversy, when Prince Louis of Battenberg was forced to resign as First Sea Lord in October 1914 due to an unreasonable public clamour against his German birth and German name. The

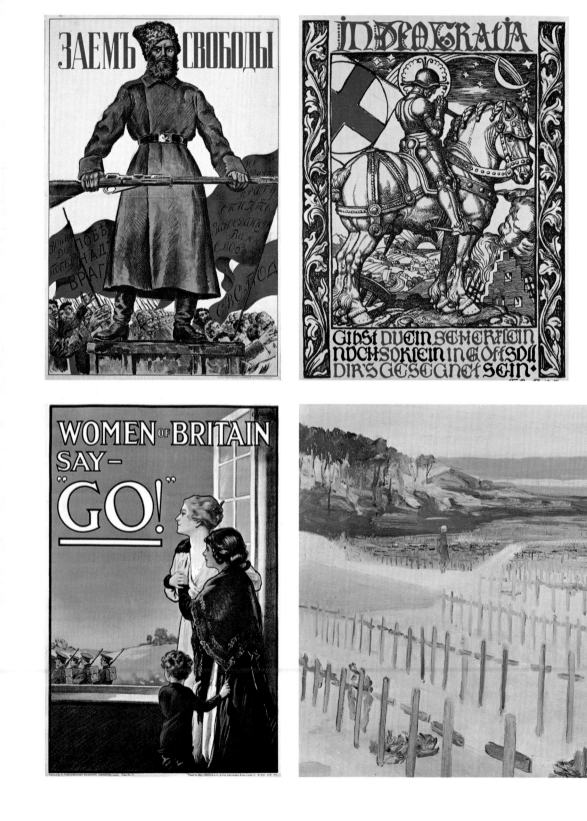

War posters of the belligerent nations emphasised the call of duty and the appeal of military glory.
LEFT A German poster by Boehle promising God's blessing upon the humblest subscriber to the war loan.
FAR LEFT A Russian war loan poster.
BELOW LEFT A recruitment poster in Britain.

The reality of trenches and graveyards was very different.
ABOVE 'Existence' by Paul Nash.
LEFT 'The Cemetery, Etaples, 1919' by Sir John Lavery.

The High Street, Poplar, during the anti-German
riots in the East End, when shops with German
names were looted and the names torn down.

ebullient Lord Fisher was appointed in his place, though misgivings were felt throughout the service. Still, with Kitchener as Secretary of State for War, and 'Jackie' Fisher at the Admiralty, two outsize personalities were controlling the Empire's forces.

The scandalous uprooting of Louis of Battenberg was symptomatic of the vituperative and near hysterical atmosphere which characterised the early months of the war, and which continued to manifest itself throughout the conflict. Anything German was automatically a target for the attentions of overzealous patriots. East End shopkeepers with German names had their premises looted, and King George found himself under pressure to expunge the name of his cousin the Kaiser, who held the honorary command of a British regiment, from the Army List. Under protest, the King agreed to the dropping of the Kaiser's name, as well as that of his son the Crown Prince. Soon other demands were made upon the King. One was that the eight enemy rulers and princes who were Knights of the Garter should have their banners removed from St George's Chapel at Windsor; this the King eventually agreed to only after strong prompting by the Prime Minister. Another cause of agitation was that some foreign princes, like the Duke of Brunswick and the King of Hanover, were still theoretically members of the British royal House. King George rightly considered these matters too trivial and undignified to be worth the attention of Parliament and the government, but Asquith eventually appointed a committee of the House of Lords to investigate the matter, and in 1917 a Titles Deprivation Act was introduced.

The King had shown his habitual commonsense in the face of these petty demands. Generally, however, the country was prone to rumour-mongering of the most ludicrous sort. Typical of such flights of fancy was the *Times* report of the Russian troops, 'little short of a million', that had marched from Aberdeen through England in order to reach the western front. The troops were allegedly identified by the snow on their boots! Not surprisingly, the British chose to believe the best of the allies, the worst of the enemy. At the battle of Mons, for example, it was claimed that an angel had lent spiritual sustenance to the British Expeditionary Force. As for the German troops, they were credited with behaviour that would have been

A British poster which shows the virulence of war propaganda.

more appropriate for the hordes of Atilla the Hun; they had allegedly raped nuns and cut off the hands of Belgian infants by the bucketful.

Xenophobia was not one of King George's weaknesses, and he refused to be swept along on the wave of anti-German feeling. Sturdily committed to his people's cause, and with no particular linguistic or cultural affinity with any European nation, he nevertheless had scant sympathy with the hatred of Germany expressed in the *Daily Mail* or in the ultra-patriotic columns of Horatio Bottomley's *John Bull*. Yet in December 1914, he reacted angrily to news that German warships had bombarded the Yorkshire coast, '& shelled Hartlepool and Scarborough for 40 minutes, doing considerable damage, killing about 40 women, children & civilians and maiming & wounding about 400. This is German *Kultur*.'

Although the King continued to be keenly moved by such examples of his subjects' sufferings, and though very much aware of the tremendous cost of the war in terms of human dignity and happiness, the face he presented to the public was confident and cheerful; concerned, but never morbid. As a constitutional monarch, his wartime role was essentially the same as in times of peace, except that the demands made upon him were much intensified. With his ministers he continued to 'advise, encourage and warn'; in the last resort, he was bound to accept their policies, as always, but the mass of official documentation that he saw, and the detailed and often im-passioned private letters of exhortation and complaint that he received, made his opinions count for something.

His public duties assumed a new significance. As the head of state, in whose name armies marched and battleships put to sea, he was the fulcrum of patriotism. During the war, King George paid seven visits to British naval bases, held 450 inspections, conferred some 50,000 decorations with his own hands, visited 300 hospitals, and frequently toured the industrial regions, training grounds, and bombed areas. He also went five times to visit the armies in France.

The King's two eldest sons also did their duty. The Prince of Wales served as aide-de-camp on the personal staff of the Commander-in-Chief in France, and subsequently as a staff officer in the Mediterranean and Italy. But it was considered inadvisable to allow the Prince to play a fuller part in the fighting. Lord Kitchener put the position plainly, if uncharitably, when he pointed out that, although it would not matter overmuch if the heir to the throne was killed or wounded, his capture would be extraordinarily awkward for the Allies. Prince Edward apparently chafed at the restrictions thus imposed upon him, and did his best to escape from them. His brother Prince Albert had more luck, and continued his service in the Royal Navy, even to the extent of taking part, as a sub-lieutenant on HMS *Collingwood*, in the Battle of Jutland in 1916.

Well before the Battle of Jutland, however, the Liberal government had run into grave difficulties over the conduct of the war. Asquith continued to leave individual ministers to operate with virtually the same amount of administrative freedom as in peacetime. Churchill, at the Admiralty, and Lloyd George, at the Treasury, were fertile in ideas, and favoured delivering a quick knock-out blow against the Central Powers well beyond the stagnant western theatre of war. Kitchener, mute and prestigious, had few masterstrokes of strategic initiative to present to his Cabinet colleagues, but still managed to overawe them with his occasional flashes of insight and the cold stare of his intensely blue eyes. Eventually, Kitchener backed Churchill's plan for a naval assault, supported by the army, against the Dardanelles and Constantinople. The theory was that a successful attack would destroy Turkey as an ally of Germany and Austria-Hungary, and then somehow lead to the collapse of the Central Powers, at a trivial cost in men and money. By May 1915 this grand, though ill-considered, campaign had failed. The Royal Navy had not forced the Dardanelle straits as planned, and when British, Australian and New Zealand troops at last landed on the Gallipoli peninsula they were soon pinned down in a line of trenches as rigid as any on the western front. The Cabinet had, in effect, merely opened another war of non-movement in even more inhospitable conditions than those in France and Flanders.

As the Dardanelles initiative was petering out in the east, a grave scandal was brewing in the west. Between 10 March and 25 May 1915, the British armies under General Sir John French fought three inconclusive battles at Neuve Chapelle, Second Ypres and Aubers Ridge. French complained, rightly, that his

OPPOSITE King George standing amid the desolation of Wytschaete Ridge in 1917. During the war the King visited the entrenched armies five times.

132

An HMSO poster advising
the public to learn how
to distinguish
hostile aircraft.

efforts had been hampered by lack of shells for the artillery. In Britain, Lord Northcliffe, Press baron and owner of the *Daily Mail* and *The Times*, thundered out his denunciations. The shell shortage scandal embarrassed the government; the Conservative and Unionist leaders were hungry for office; the Irish Nationalists had no cause to sustain the Liberals now that the Home Rule Act had been put into cold storage for the duration of the war; Labour wished to assert their Parliamentary independence of the Liberals.

On 17 May 1915, Asquith formed a coalition government, though one in which the Conservatives were markedly junior partners. The Conservative leader Bonar Law went to the Colonial Office, which was hardly the choicest of political plums; Balfour took the Admiralty, though not himself much of a sea-dog; the Ulster militant Edward Carson became Attorney General. There were other gestures of unity, when Arthur Henderson, for Labour, was made President of the Board of Education, and Redmond the Irish Nationalist leader was offered, but refused, a Cabinet post. Haldane, however, resigned as Lord Chancellor because of his allegedly pro-German sentiments. Two of the most dynamic members of the Liberal administration received contrasting treatment: Winston Churchill was demoted from the Admiralty to the Duchy of Lancaster, thus partly paying the price for the Dardanelles failure but cast down chiefly because of the hatred felt for him within the Conservative party, as a turncoat and class-traitor; Lloyd George, however, was given the newly-created Ministry of Munitions, from which vantage point he was to emerge as the man who could win the war and rally the people.

Thus fell the last Liberal government of modern times – not with a bang, not even with a whimper (except from the party organisation in the constituencies), but with a shuffling of ministerial positions. The conduct of the war went from bad to worse, though Lloyd George at the Ministry of Munitions showed a sure grasp of priorities, ensuring the manufacture of large quantities of machine-guns, beginning to satisfy the demand for shells and establishing extremely cordial relations with organised labour. But from the theatres of war the news was sombre. The Germans began their U-boat campaign against merchant ships, a dramatic counterstroke to the Royal

Navy's blockade of Germany. Zeppelins bombed London, though causing only light casualties. A further assault was made at Gallipoli; it was as unsuccessful as the first. There was no breakthrough on the western front. 1915 ended even more badly than it had begun.

King George had lent his government what support he could during these trying times. In response to Lloyd George's conviction that drunkenness among the munitions workers was hampering the war effort, he became a teetotaller, though confiding in his diary that 'I hate doing it, but hope it will do good.' The example of royal abstinence was not, however, universally followed, and brewers and spirits manufacturers continued to rake in handsome profits! More practical was the backing the King gave Asquith over the controversial Military Service Bill which eventually became law in January 1916. By the latter part of 1915, it was evident that the continuing slaughter in the trenches made some form of military conscription unavoidable. The Prime Minister wished to ensure that all single men between the ages of eighteen and forty would be available for service if needed. But the proposed legislation split the Cabinet, provoking Sir John Simon to resign as Home Secretary and even ranging Sir Edward Grey with Reginald McKenna against the Prime Minister. King George was dismayed at this division between Liberal members of the coalition government, and told Asquith that 'he would stand by him and support him, even if all his colleagues were to leave'. Thus sustained, the Prime Minister was able to win over his recalcitrant ministers.

The King's visits to the western front began in November 1914. Queen Mary was persuaded that it was not woman's work, but still wrote sorrowfully on 29 November:

> My own darling Georgie dear, I felt very sad at seeing you go today on your important mission, without me, for all these years I have thank God been able to accompany you on all important journeys during our married life, so I feel it rather having to stay at home. I think you were quite right to go and it will be such a help & encouragement to officers & men in their arduous work.... God bless & protect you my own darling Georgie dear ever your loving wife – May.

While the King toured the encampments and battlefields in France and Flanders, he exchanged daily letters with Queen

OPPOSITE The U-boat sinking aroused much anti-German feeling in the United States and this picture of a drowned woman and her baby was an emotional appeal to Americans to enlist.

ENLIST

Fred Spear

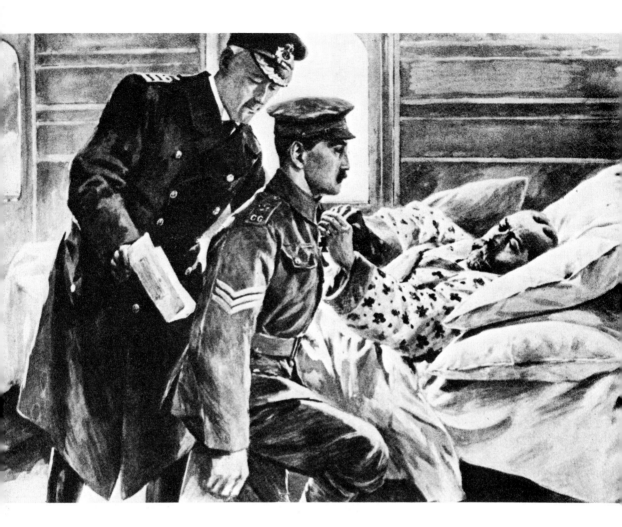

The King in a hospital train after his fall decorates Lance-Sergeant Oliver Brooks with the Victoria Cross. On the left is Sir Charles Cust, his equerry.

Mary. Naturally the Queen feared for his safety, and in October 1915, during his second visit, he indeed suffered a serious injury, though not as the result of enemy action. The accident occurred when King George's chestnut mare reared in fright at the cheers of men of the Royal Flying Corps and fell, pinning her rider to the ground. The King fractured his pelvis in two places, and suffered severe bruising; it is some indication of his distress that he admitted in his diary 'They picked me up and took me back to Aire in the motor.... I suffered agonies all the way.... During October 29, 30 and 31 I suffered great pain and hardly slept at all.' The King mended slowly, but was subsequently liable to suffer discomfort from his injuries. In this way, he became one of the permanent war-wounded, and this

new strain upon his health undoubtedly contributed to the irascibility of his later years.

A more constructive result of the King's visits was his conviction that the British Commander-in-Chief, Sir John French, should be replaced. Not only was French, understandably as it happened, failing to produce results on the battlefield, but he was at loggerheads with Lord Kitchener, Sir Douglas Haig, commander of the First British Army, and Sir William Robertson, his own Chief of Staff. The King did not think highly of French, remarking in May 1915, 'I don't think he is particularly clever & he has an awful temper. Whether he is now suffering from the strain of the campaign or from a swollen head I don't know, but he is behaving in a very odd

General Weygand describes battle movements to the King on the Belgian front. General Foch is on the right of the King and General Haig on the left of Weygand.

139

way, which adds to my many anxieties.' In October 1915, he noted that 'several of the most important Generals have entirely lost confidence in the C. in C. and they assured me that it was universal & that he must go, otherwise we shall never win this war. This has been my opinion for some time.' When, in December, French seemed disinclined to resign, though under pressure to do so, the King urged Asquith to press the point, and was delighted when Sir Douglas Haig was able to succeed to the command of British forces on the western front. Haig had long been a good friend of the King; he knew that he could rely on his sovereign's support even in the most adverse conditions, and in return he kept the King supplied with a great deal of information, even gossip, concerning his command.

The year of 1916 provided little to cheer the Allies, and 'war weariness' became a distinguishable phenomenon. Sir Douglas Haig's promotion did not produce exhilarating British victories on the western front. Indeed, in July, the great offensive on the Somme, which was supposed to smash like a battering-ram through the German defences, began with 76,000 British casualties on the first day. By November, when the mud made the co-ordinated movements of armies impossible, 420,000 British losses had been sustained. This slaughter in the west was partly offset by the increasingly successful tactics of a brilliant young officer, T. E. Lawrence, in rallying Arab tribesmen against their Turkish overlords in the Middle East; but in Mesopotamia a more orthodox campaign led to the surrender of 10,000 British troops in April.

Even at sea, there was no twentieth-century Trafalgar to stir the blood, though the long-awaited clash between the British and German fleets took place at the end of May. The Battle of Jutland was, however, a curious encounter which occupied five minutes of evening light. Prince Albert, who was on board HMS *Collingwood*, gave a first-hand account to his parents, telling them that 'The hands behaved splendidly and all of them in the best of spirits as their heart's desire had at last been granted, which was to be in action with the Germans.... It was certainly a great experience to have been through and it shows that we are at war and that the Germans can fight if they want.' The losses sustained by both fleets certainly showed that the Germans could fight, for the Royal Navy lost three battlecruisers, three

OPPOSITE T. E. Lawrence in the desert.

OVERLEAF A field dressing station on the Somme.

140

armoured cruisers and eight destroyers, while the enemy's High Seas Fleet lost one battleship, one battlecruiser, four light cruisers and five destroyers. Still, the German fleet had fled for shelter, and emerged only once more, and then to no effect, during the rest of the war. The British blockade of Germany continued as before, while for their part the Germans waged an increasingly successful U-boat campaign.

The bitter feelings aroused by the German U-boat sinkings prompted the Cabinet to consider in April 1915 imposing 'differential treatment' upon prisoners-of-war taken from captured submarines. King George, though deploring 'the general conduct of the Germans throughout this war', made it plain that 'he deprecates the idea of reprisals and retaliation; he has always hoped that at the end of the war we shall as a Nation stand before the world as having conducted it as far as possible with humanity and like gentlemen'. The King's honourable protest went unheeded until the Germans retaliated in kind by placing thirty-nine British officers in solitary confinement; henceforth, captured German submarine crews were accorded the same treatment as other prisoners-of-war.

On the home front Britain suffered the acute embarrassment of the Dublin Easter rising. Members of the extremist Irish Volunteer movement seized the Dublin general post office and proclaimed the Irish Republic. It took four days to restore order at the cost of 100 British and 450 Irish lives. It was a small-scale disturbance compared with the massive conflict in Europe, but of potent symbolism. Above all, it was an embarrassment for a nation which claimed to have gone to war to protect the national identity of 'gallant little Belgium'. Indeed, contrary to general belief, the Empire did not stand enthusiastically at Britain's side throughout the entire war. At the outset, in South Africa, an Afrikaner, pro-German rebellion had to be put down; French Canadians were demonstrably slow to volunteer and bitterly opposed the attempt to introduce conscription in 1917; the Australians actually voted against conscription in a referendum in the same year.

Even in Britain the introduction of conscription in 1916 provoked bitter debate. The fiasco on the Somme helped turn some of the more literate observers into trenchant critics of military incompetence; poets like Wilfrid Owen, Robert

Graves and Siegfried Sassoon wrote verse that contrasted sharply with the earlier rhapsodising of Rupert Brooke. The common soldier expressed his despair and endurance and cynicism more racily in the marching-songs which became as immortal as the work of the war poets:

> We are Fred Karno's army,
> The ragtime infantry.
> We cannot fight, we cannot shoot,
> What bleeding use are we?
> And when we get to Berlin
> The Kaiser he will say,
> 'Hoch! Hoch! Mein Gott!
> What a bloody rotten lot!
> What a bloody rotten lot are they!'

As 1916 ended, the British people could look back over a year of set-back and frustration. Even that totem of martial spirit, Lord Kitchener, had died, drowned in the North Sea on a mission to Russia. Victory seemed no nearer than two years' earlier; indeed, with Russia flagging and the French massively engaged at Verdun, it seemed further away than ever. Asquith had at no time seemed capable of winning the war; Lloyd George, on the contrary, believed that, like some latterday Earl of Chatham, he could do just that. In December 1916, a palace revolution occurred: Lloyd George threw Asquith over and rallied Conservatives and Labour to his cause. His new coalition government included Bonar Law, Balfour, Curzon, Arthur Henderson and Alfred Milner; Grey, Lord Crewe and six Liberal ministers resigned with Asquith. A war which had involved the people more than any other, both on the battle-field and on the industrial front (on which women too had played a vital part), was now led by the first Prime Minister to come from the people. It was appropriate enough.

Lloyd George set about streamlining the administration. He created a select War Cabinet which effectively ran the war, and from 1917 included even a Dominion statesman, Jan Smuts – a former Boer commander. He brought the Dominion and Indian leaders into the intimate workings of the government at the Imperial War Conference of 1917. He did not leave the generals to run the war, but badgered them, maybe conspired

The battle of Passchendaele. Canadian troops of the Second Division carrying duckboards towards Passchendaele with prisoners and wounded straggling in.

against some and, in a number of cases, openly despised them. Lloyd George also promoted the positive involvement of the state in the economy and in the lives of the people. This 'war socialism' was not without its teething problems, but it was at least a positive move towards the centralisation essential to the deployment of national resources.

The new Prime Minister was both inspired and lucky. His inspiration provided, for example, the antidote to the alarming U-boat sinkings of allied shipping in the Atlantic – the convoy. His luck held even when in 1917 the Russian Revolution caused the Tsar to abdicate and struck a grievous blow at the

146

Allied cause in the eastern front, for a month later the United States entered the war in reaction to Germany's campaign of unrestricted submarine warfare. One giant had been exchanged for another, though an inefficient and ailing one for one of boundless vitality and enormous industrial strength. The war was not yet won, but it now appeared much more winnable.

King George viewed Lloyd George's accession to the premiership with apprehension. He continued to admire Asquith, and to distrust his successor's more unorthodox methods. While respecting Lloyd George's great abilities, he regretted that a far from cordial relationship developed between the Prime Minister and Sir Douglas Haig. But the momentous events that unfolded in Russia three months after Lloyd George's successful bid for power touched him at a deeper personal level. His cousin the Kaiser was head of the state of hostile Germany, now another cousin, the Tsar Nicholas II, had been cast down. Despite his close personal friendship with the Tsar, however, the King sensibly saw that it would be inexpedient to offer him sanctuary in Britain. He had cause to regret this decision when the Tsar and his family were murdered in 1918 after the Bolsheviks had come to power in October 1917. Mrs Asquith recorded the King's reaction to the murders, 'I had tears in my eyes – and have still – when he spoke of the vindictive and unnecessary murder of the poor Czar and I was moved to deepest admiration by his revolt over this alien stunt.'

The landing of General Pershing in June 1917 with the first units of the United States army gave King George the opportunity to address the American staff officers and their leader in forthright terms, saying 'It has always been my dream that the two English-speaking nations should some day be united in a great cause, and today my dream is realised. Together we are fighting for the greatest cause that people can fight. The Anglo-Saxon race must save civilisation.' But in March 1918, it looked, for a moment, as if the American troops had not arrived in sufficiently large numbers to hold back a crushing German offensive in the west. General Ludendorff, the hero of Tannenberg, waited until his army's numbers had been swollen by German divisions transferred from the eastern front after the Treaty of Brest Litovsk had ended the war with Bolshevik Russia; he then hurled them against the French and British lines. He achieved alarming breakthroughs and caused some despondency among the Allies. King George even wrote to his mother, Queen Alexandra, 'we must be courageous & go on to the end, however long it may take, as I shall never submit to those brutal Germans & I am sure the British nation is of the same opinion'.

'I shall never submit to those brutal Germans'

Fortunately, the British nation was never put to the ultimate test. By the middle of July, British, French and American counter-attacks were pushing back the spent German forces. October opened with allied forces smashing through the Siegfried line into open country. A new German government

148

was in office and had been advised by Ludendorff to seek an armistice. In the Middle East, General Allenby was clearing the last Turkish army out of Arab territory. Turkey capitulated on 30 October, Austria-Hungary on 4 November, and on 9 November a German republic was proclaimed from the steps of the Reichstag. The next day the Kaiser crossed into the Netherlands and exile. On 11 November, the armistice was signed. The war to end wars was over.

Land for Heroes 1918-24

T HE NEWS OF THE ARMISTICE ran like lightning throughout the British Isles. Within minutes, crowds flocked into the streets of London and other great cities, their jubilation composed equally of triumph at Britain's victory and relief that the drudgery and waste of war was over. A great upsurge of patriotic rejoicing flooded round the royal family; for five days after the armistice, King George and Queen Mary drove through the streets of London past massed, waving crowds. When the King reviewed a gathering of disabled servicemen in Hyde Park, he recorded that 'There were between 30,000 and 35,000 present: they were most enthusiastic & in riding down the lines they broke through & came round me to shake hands. I was nearly pulled off my horse.' Towards the end of November, he visited the battle areas in France and Belgium where 'At each place I got out & walked through the troops who cheered me. It was not stiff, the men often following me through the town. A fine drizzle which was pretty wetting and plenty of mud.'

The King's tireless devotion to the official routine of inspections, visits to industrial regions and the general encouragement of his people's war effort, thus received a satisfying reward in his evident popularity. Lloyd George subsequently paid an equally handsome tribute when he wrote that 'There can be no question that one outstanding reason for the high level of loyalty and patriotic effort which the people of this country maintained was the attitude and conduct of King George.'

The euphoria of victory could not, however, altogether obliterate memories of earlier criticisms levelled at the monarchy. In April 1917, doubtless stimulated by the Russian Revolution, H. G. Wells had publicly advocated republicanism, and had subsequently referred to the 'alien and uninspiring court'. Well-informed contemporaries realised, of course, that the royal residences were hardly Renaissance Courts bursting with eager enquiry and high-thinking, and Max Beerbohm was later to ridicule the apparently pedestrian intellectual qualities of King George and Queen Mary in a poem (or one-act play) written for private circulation and entitled *Ballade Tragique à Double Refrain*; it is alleged that these biting and patronising verses deferred Beerbohm's knighthood until 1939:

PREVIOUS PAGES
Lloyd George addressing a crowd at Lampeter Station in Wales, 1919.

152

Armistice scenes in London, 1918. The King
found the calls to 'Hang the Kaiser' most
distressing and was very relieved when
the Dutch government refused to hand him over.

153

SCENE *A room in Windsor Castle*
TIME *The Present*
(Enter a Lady-in-Waiting and a Lord-in-Waiting)

SHE:
Slow pass the hours, ah, passing slow;
My doom is worse than anything
Conceived by Edgar Allan Poe:
The Queen is duller than the King.
  HE:
Lady, your mind is wandering,
You babble what you do not mean;
Remember, to your heartening,
The King is duller than the Queen.
  SHE:
No, most emphatically, no
To one firm-rooted fact I cling
In my now chronic vertigo:
The Queen is duller than the King,
  HE:
Lady, you lie. Last evening
I found him with a rural dean
Talking of District Visiting....
The King is duller than the Queen.
  SHE:
At any rate he doesn't sew;
You don't see him embellishing
Yard after yard of calico....
The Queen is duller than the King.
Oh, to have been an underling
To (say) the Empress Josephine.
  HE:
Enough of your self-pitying;
The King is duller than the Queen.
  SHE:
The Queen is duller than the King.
  HE:
Death, then, for you shall have no sting.
*(Stabs her, and as she falls dead produces
phial from breast-pocket of coat)*
Nevertheless, sweet friend strychnine,
The King – is – duller than – the Queen.
(Expires in horrible agony)

The King's reaction to H. G. Well's slighting remark in 1917, however, was very much in character, and perfectly accurate: 'I may be uninspiring,' he said, 'but I'll be damned if I'm an alien'. There was, indeed, little that was alien about a monarch who could easily have spent his life as an officer in the Royal Navy or as a Norfolk squire, except his family names. Conscious of the Teutonic ring of 'Saxe-Coburg-Gotha,' the King sought a less offensive name for the royal House in 1917. Happily rejecting the suggestion of the Royal College of Heralds that the choice lay between 'Wipper' and 'Wettin', and advised to avoid Tudor and Stuart, the King eventually settled on 'Windsor', which was rather indistinctly connected with Edward III.

More urgent matters, however, faced the nation in November 1918, and the re-ordering of society and the economy seemed obvious priorities. The war had left many scars, though not all the wounds had gone deep. Three quarters of a million Britons had been killed during the war; yet the net loss per annum was less than the average outward movement of emigrants in the years 1912–13. The civilian population, in contrast to that of the Second World War, had endured slight casualties, but had suffered some deprivation in terms of the quality and supply of consumer goods, food and certain services. There was also an acute housing shortage. On the other hand, the war had created conditions of full employment, and wages had eventually come close to catching up the cost of living. Many industrialists had done very well indeed.

But, whether adversely or profitably, the war seemed to have affected all citizens – not just through the casualty lists, or the one and a half million men crippled by gassing or wounds, or by the new phenomenon of shell-shocked war veterans; there were experiences more universal, though infinitely less disturbing, than death and maiming on the battlefield. From February 1918, for example, food rationing was introduced; the state also undertook fresh responsibilities in the field of social welfare, almost cosseting workers in some key industries and taking unprecedented care of servicemen's wives and families. Although the disruption to civilian life was within tolerable limits, nearly all citizens could feel that they had made some sacrifice in the cause of winning the war. Thus, when Lloyd

The King's round of visits, inspections and reviews continued unabated after the war.
RIGHT Silver Badge men in Hyde Park break ranks to shake hands with the King.
LEFT King George talking to a young worker during his visit to Sunderland.
BELOW RIGHT The King visits allotments on Clapham Common.

George promised a post-war land fit for heroes, there were other heroes and heroines who had served on the domestic front and who also expected to share in the spoils of victory.

What exactly these spoils were to consist of was not clear. Women over thirty-five years old got the vote in 1918, but those under that age who had played an equally important part in the war effort did not. All adult males were enfranchised at the same time. Servicemen expected rapid demobilisation and re-employment, but in the early weeks of 1919 discontent at the rate of demobilisation led to riots in Glasgow and Belfast, and the burning down of the Luton town-hall, while in Calais there was an uncomfortable mutiny. A post-war economic boom solved the re-employment problem, and by November 1919, there were only 300,000 unemployed, a tolerable enough figure for the times. The average man who had stayed at home and done his job probably expected the government somehow to hold down price rises, encourage the building of new houses and see to reasonable wage settlements. These proved to be high hopes.

Before putting such matters to the test, however, Lloyd George fought a General Election at the end of 1918. Even before the armistice, he had discussed the situation with Bonar Law, his Coalition colleague, and had approached the King for a dissolution of Parliament. King George had showed little enthusiasm for an immediate election which would almost certainly cash in on the mood of public contentment at winning the war. He reminded the Prime Minister that the 'Khaki' election of 1900, which had been conducted when victory had seemed ensured in the Boer War, had 'brought back the Unionists with a large majority and kept them in power on what was really a fictitious vote, and ended in ruining them and keeping them out of Office ever since'. Having thus exercised his constitutional right to 'warn' his Prime Minister, the King nonetheless granted Lloyd George a dissolution.

The General Election of 1918 returned Lloyd George to power as the man who had won the war. Yet the basis of his support in the House of Commons was extremely unsatisfactory for a man who had once framed the 'People's Budget'. Although the Coalition won a sweeping victory, 339 of their 533 members were Conservative and Unionist; Lloyd George could not govern without Bonar Law's support, since his 136 Coalition Liberals were merely one sixth of the total number of MPS. Moreover, the decimation of the Asquithian Liberals, of whom only 26 were returned, denied Lloyd George the long-term prospect of reuniting the Liberal party and perhaps forming a new coalition with Labour. Asquith, who lost his seat at East Fife, had denounced the certificate of endorsement which Lloyd George and Law had sent to Coalition candidates as resulting in a 'Coupon Election', which thus sounded like an unworthy compact. But the 'coupon' was to prove Lloyd George's political death-warrant.

The Prime Minister flung himself into the massive tasks of post-war government, particularly peace-making and domestic reconstruction. At every turn, he found his freedom of action hampered by his need to placate the Conservatives. A more exacting peace treaty with Germany, hostility towards Soviet Russia, intransigence over Ireland and a tougher line with the trade unions were all part of the price Lloyd George paid to keep in power. It is to his credit that his dextrous, yet frequently oblique, approach to these problems achieved more conciliation than often appeared possible at the outset.

With the General Election won, the Prime Minister busied himself with peace-making. Unfortunately, during the election campaign, he had committed himself both to bringing the Kaiser to trial as a war criminal, and to squeezing the last penny out of Germany in reparations for the war. Trying the Kaiser (or 'hanging the Kaiser', as some patriots advocated) was a difficult and intrinsically worthless gambit. King George felt deep misgivings over the whole affair and it was a relief to him, and doubtless to Lloyd George, when the Netherlands' government resolutely refused to hand over the exiled Kaiser to the Allies. Nor did the King relish the harsh peace terms which were finally dictated to Germany and, to a lesser extent, Austria. Indeed, he felt it incumbent upon him to intervene on a few occasions and make his views known to his ministers. Thus, in November 1919, he wrote to the Foreign Office expressing 'shock at the condition of things in Vienna', and advocating 'the prompt adoption of some measures for the provision of those necessaries of life which, owing to the conditions of the Peace Treaty, seem to be withheld from the people, especially at a time when the rigours of an early winter have to be faced'.

Apart from saddling Germany with unrealistic debts and stripping her of the appurtenances of 'great power' status, the Allies went on to dismember the German Empire; they also rationalised the break-up of the Austrian and Turkish Empires. There was, however, no vulgar handing out of territory. The principle of national self-determination was applied in central Europe, and fitfully in the Middle East. Elsewhere, ex-enemy territories were declared mandates of the newly-formed League of Nations and handed out respectably to the victors. In this way, Britain was able to disclaim brash territorial annexation and at the same time effectively absorb countries like Tanganyika, Mesopotamia and Palestine. The British Dominions of Australia, New Zealand and South Africa got their lion-cubs' share of mandated territory as well. By a quirk of history, therefore, Britain, who had apparently fought the war at least in part for the rights of small nations, extended her Empire by an area of almost a million square miles containing thirteen million inhabitants.

One part of the Empire, however, longed to break away. The Sinn Fein party had swept the electoral board in southern Ireland in 1918, and the administration of the southern counties was effectively in nationalist hands. In January 1919, the Sinn Fein MPs met as the Irish *Dail*, or Parliament, and elected Eamon De Valera President of the Irish Republic. The extremists of the Irish Republican Army, backed by money from sympathisers in the United States, began a guerilla campaign to drive the British out and to unite all Ireland. British statesmen shied away from the logistical and moral implications of reconquest, which would have involved an army of a hundred thousand and, doubtless, international condemnation. As it was, there were fifty thousand British troops in Ireland, and enough harsh criticism from foreign powers, particularly the United States. In 1920, the British government invited more obloquy for its use of auxiliary troops, or 'Black and Tans', whose name became a byword for terror and brutality.

King George disapproved of these methods. In May 1921 he wrote, via his secretary Lord Stamfordham, to Sir Hamar Greenwood, the Chief Secretary for Ireland, that 'The King does ask himself, and he asks you, if this policy of reprisals is to be continued and, if so, to where will it lead Ireland and us all. It seems to His Majesty that in punishing the guilty we are inflicting punishment no less severe upon the innocent.' A year later, an American newspaper alleged that the King had said 'I cannot have my people killed in this manner.' King George was hardly a supporter of republicanism, nor of the Sinn Fein, but it is clear that he considered himself still responsible for the safety of his Irish subjects, and that he reacted strongly against the outrages being committed in his name.

In 1921, the King was able to exercise a personal influence on Irish affairs which was both unusual for a constitutional monarch and plainly effective. In 1920, Lloyd George, seeking, as so often, for an ingenious solution to an intractable problem, had devised a new Government of Ireland Act. The provisions of the Act sought the best of both worlds; both Ulster and the south were to have Home Rule *and* representation at Westminster; a Council of Ireland was somehow to draw both sections closer together. Neither the north nor the south cared wholeheartedly for the Act, though Ulster snatched at the chance of a Parliament in Belfast. King George insisted, despite the risk of assassination, on opening this new Parliament in person. The speech which he made on that occasion was to bring some substantial improvement in Anglo-Irish relations.

The origins of the King's Belfast speech owe much to the fertile imagination of General Smuts, then Prime Minister of South Africa. In June 1921, he was in London for the Imperial Conference. Smuts had been through the trauma of the Boer War of 1899–1902, but had seen the majority of the Afrikaner people accept Dominion status within the Empire. He believed that if the King's speech promised southern Ireland Dominion status too, then the way towards reconciliation would be opened up. The speech to the new Ulster Parliament was less specific on this point than Smuts had proposed, but ended with the words 'the future lies in the hands of the Irish people. May this historic gathering be the prelude to the day in which the Irish people, north and south, under one Parliament or two, as those Parliaments may themselves decide, shall work together in common love for Ireland upon the sure foundation of mutual justice and respect.'

At first, the response to the King's speech was excellent. De

De Valera seeks help for the Irish Republican Army at Los Angeles in 1919.

Valera agreed to negotiate with the British authorities, and a truce was signed within three weeks. During subsequent negotiations, however, the Irish quibbled over the precise form of Dominion status and over other British proposals. One of De Valera's written statements caused the King to dismiss it as 'a hopeless document, written by a dreamer and a visionary with nothing practical about it'. But Lloyd George managed to break the deadlock. The 'Welsh wizard' had a new trick up his sleeve. He renewed negotiations and managed first to give the impression that Ulster would be put under Dublin for a limited period, then to threaten an end to the truce and renewed hostilities, and finally to suggest that Ulster could be made so unworkable a unit that it would gladly seek re-union with the south.

This approach, so reminiscent of the fluctuations between 'coercion' and 'kindness' in earlier days, worked. At least, the *Dail* and the Westminster Parliament had both approved an Anglo-Irish treaty by January 1922. But De Valera resigned as President, and a large section of the I.R.A fought on for the idea of a united republic until 1923. The Irish Free State, however, came into being as a Dominion, albeit one of truculent bearing and scant sympathy for the principles of imperial co-operation. The British had, for a time at least, got the Irish problem off their backs, but only at the expense of a new and unenthusiastic member of the self-governing Commonwealth.

The fact that Lloyd George had provided a solution in Ireland did him surprisingly little good at home. Those on the left remembered the 'Black and Tans'; his Conservative and Unionist allies had seen the union dissolved. This alone did not bring the Prime Minister down. Social reform had been expected after the sacrifices of the Great War; little came between 1918 and 1922. The reasons were straightforward enough: Lloyd George's Conservative allies set no great store by such a programme, and the colossal national debt that had been incurred by the cost of the war inhibited lavish public spending. Trade union discontent was increasingly expressed, most ominously for the government, in the 'triple alliance' between miners, railwaymen and dockers. In 1920, the threat of a general strike apparently prevented the government from intervening against Bolshevik Russia in her war with Poland.

The emergence of powerful new trade union leaders like J.H. Thomas and Ernest Bevin made organised labour more difficult to browbeat, though the 1921 miners' strike was broken. Generally, wages fell during 1921, and in June unemployment passed the two million mark. The post-war economic boom was over, and so with a vengeance was Lloyd George's evocation of a promised land for heroes to live in.

The mood of disillusionment and discontent did not, however, end Lloyd George's premiership. He fell because the Conservative party would not support the Cabinet's decision in October 1922 to fight a General Election on the Coalition ticket. Lloyd George pressed for an election during the tail-end of the Chanak crisis, when Britain had announced her intention to defend the garrison of Chanak in the neutralised Dardanelles against the advancing forces of the Turkish nationalist leader, Kemal Ataturk. The Prime Minister had openly appealed to the British Dominions for military support and had received a public rebuff when Canada and South Africa had refused to act. All hopes for a common imperial foreign policy were thus torn to shreds.

But it was not only Chanak that ruined Lloyd George. The Conservative rank and file wanted an end to his Prime Ministership, and Bonar Law who had helped him to supreme power in 1916 decided to deny it to him in 1922. At a meeting of Conservative MPs at the Carlton Club, the relatively obscure President of the Board of Trade, Stanley Baldwin, denounced Lloyd George and argued that he would eventually destroy the party. Lloyd George resigned within hours of the decision. The King, who had keenly regretted Asquith's departure in 1916, now felt similarly for Lloyd George and wrote 'I am sorry he is going, but some day he will be Prime Minister again.' In fact, Lloyd George was doomed to spend the rest of his life in the political wilderness. Bonar Law took his place in 10 Downing Street, and a month later won the General Election even though nearly three million more votes were cast for the Liberals and Labour than for the Conservatives. Still, for the first time in seventeen years, the nation had a Conservative Prime Minister.

There were other novelties in Britain as the year of 1922

163

King George found his second son, Albert, Duke of York, far easier to understand than 'dear David'. He was very happy at the Duke's marriage to Lady Elizabeth Bowes-Lyon, now the Queen Mother, photographed above as they left Buckingham Palace for their honeymoon.

ended. If the rich had stayed more or less rich, and the poor had stayed poor, the social habits, dress and leisure activities of both had altered with the Great War. All social classes now smoked cigarettes rather than pipes or cigars; the lounge-suit became the working-dress of the middle classes, and the Sunday dress of the working classes; women's fashions became much less fussy, and the ideally boyish figure of the 'flapper' was clad with simplicity, while the cloche hat echoed the steel helmets of the war. In the arts, Jacob Epstein's sculptures were provoking admiration and incomprehension, more of the latter than the former; T. S. Eliot, D. H. Lawrence, James Joyce and Aldous Huxley were the great literary figures, though the masses preferred to read Edgar Wallace; the BBC had just begun its radio broadcasts which, though of variable quality, were a challenge to both the music-halls and the popular Press; the cinema, though still silent, could boast Charlie Chaplin and a host of other stars who became household names in many parts of the world, thus dwarfing the fame even of a Marie Lloyd or a George Robey.

The King was by no means in tune with all of these developments. His eldest son, however, was. In 1922, the Prince of

Wales was twenty-eight years old, unmarried, vivacious and of an independent turn of mind. King George took pride in his son's evident popularity, but in private expressed misgivings over Prince Edward's informal conduct and alleged flippancy. Prone to exercise a tight discipline over his children, he perhaps too often mistook high spirits for behaviour unbecoming to the blood royal. It is clear, though, that when his sons married, the King's attitude towards them softened, and he made great efforts to welcome their brides affably into his family. But since the Prince of Wales did not marry during his father's lifetime, he was not able to benefit from these gentler moods.

Prince Edward's official activities ought to have earned paternal approval. In 1919, he visited Newfoundland, Canada and the United States. A year later, he toured Australia and New Zealand, via the West Indies, Honolulu and Fiji, and at the end of 1921 he set out to visit India. This was a far more complex mission than his previous ones. It had been relatively easy to enrapture Australian, Canadian and even American spectators, but Indian nationalism was in the process of being mobilised by Gandhi's non-violent non-co-operation movement, and the Prince was unlikely to receive an enthusiastic welcome. Prince Edward displayed his considerable charm, tact and warmth, but his impact on the Indian people was at best transitory. Nothing more could reasonably have been expected in a situation in which the foundations of the Raj were being steadily eroded.

The essence of King George's private anxieties over his eldest son is neatly expressed in a letter he wrote to his second, more retiring, son, the Duke of York, shortly after he had married Lady Elizabeth Bowes-Lyon in 1923. The King told his second son

> You are indeed a lucky man to have such a charming and delightful wife as Elizabeth. I am sure you will both be very happy together. I trust ... that you will be as happy as Mama & I am after you have been married for 30 years.... You have always been so sensible & easy to work with & you have always been ready to listen to any advice & to agree with my opinions about people & things that I feel we have always got on very well together. Very different to dear David [the Prince of Wales].

Affairs of state, however, were soon to demand more urgent

The Prince of Wales

King George was disturbed by the dashing playboy image of the Prince of Wales (right) and did not fully appreciate the seriousness with which he took his official duties.

BELOW The Prince facing a battery of cameras during his visit to Australia in 1920.

RIGHT The Prince in
Aden, 1921.

BELOW The Prince
leaving the Cymner
pithead after a trip
into the mine.

attention than the errant Prince of Wales. Bonar Law had only recently abandoned his withdrawal from active politics on grounds of ill-health in order to cut down Lloyd George in October 1922. Within six months of taking office, the new Prime Minister left on a sea voyage to restore his failing health. On his return, his complaint was diagnosed as cancer of the throat. In May 1923, he resigned, and the King had to exercise his prerogative in the choice of a successor to the premiership. The choice was not an obvious one. Balfour was too old, Austen Chamberlain too remote, Lord Birkenhead (F. E. Smith) too provocative; Churchill was not even a Conservative, though teetering on the brink of once more becoming one. Moreover, none of the three former statesmen had joined Law's government of 'the second eleven', preferring, as willing supporters of the Lloyd George Coalition, to hold aloof.

But Lord Curzon and Stanley Baldwin were respectively Foreign Secretary and Chancellor of the Exchequer under the stricken Bonar Law. A casual observer would not have considered them serious rivals. Curzon was an aristocrat, an ex-Viceroy of India, the possessor of a powerful personality and (so he himself believed) a powerful intellect. Baldwin was the son of an ironmaster, pipe-smoking, unobtrusive, even ordinary, holding in the Chancellorship his first great office of state. Yet it was Baldwin who succeeded to the premiership – not because Law had recommended him to the King, since the outgoing Prime Minister was either too ill or too uncertain to follow established precedent and make his views clearly known, but because as a House of Commons man he seemed more appropriate to an age that claimed to be increasingly democratic than an hereditary peer with a reputation for abrasive political and administrative relationships.

Deprived of a clear recommendation from Bonar Law, the King had consulted Lord Balfour who, on more than one occasion, had found Curzon an irksome colleague. Balfour's judgment that the new Prime Minister should be a member of the House of Commons confirmed the King's own feelings. Lord Stamfordham, the King's Private Secretary, was given the unenviable task of breaking the news to Curzon, who replied that the decision was 'the greatest blow and slur upon him and his public career, now at its summit, that he could ever have conceived'. Privately he expressed the view that Baldwin was a man of 'the utmost insignificance'.

As it happened, Baldwin's first administration lasted for only seven months, during which time its only notable achievement was the enactment of Neville Chamberlain's Housing Act, and even that did little to improve working-class housing conditions. Then, in October 1923, perhaps encouraged by the promptings of the Imperial Conference then in session, Baldwin announced that he wished to introduce a policy of fiscal protection in order to combat unemployment more effectively. This was merely a rehashing of Joseph Chamberlain's old warcry that 'Tariff reform means work for all!' It was a no more accurate exhortation in 1923 than in 1906. A General Election must now necessarily be fought on an issue which Balfour had dropped in 1910 and even Bonar Law, the arch-protectionist, in 1922.

The election campaign achieved some reforming of party ranks. Austen Chamberlain came over to Baldwin, as did other Conservatives who had earlier preferred Lloyd George to Law. The Asquithian Liberals could unite with the Lloyd George Liberals in defence of free trade. Though Baldwin struggled to disassociate protection from higher food prices and declared against 'stomach taxes', many of the electorate failed to believe him. The election in December 1923 resulted in over ninety Conservative losses, while the Liberals gained forty and Labour fifty. The new House of Commons consisted of 258 Conservatives, 159 Liberals and 191 Labour men. When the House reassembled, the Conservatives would be the largest party, but vulnerable to instant defeat if the two opposition parties voted against them.

This was an unprecedented constitutional situation in which King George was once more destined to play an important part. He began by refusing to let Baldwin resign immediately, and suggesting that he 'ought not to accept the verdict of the Polls, except as expressed by the representatives of the Electorate across the floor of the House of Commons'. Since defeat in the Commons was certain to come, the King would then be obliged to send for Ramsay MacDonald as the leader of the largest opposition party. Conservative and even some Liberal reaction to this prospect was at best confused, at worst unconstitutional.

Various schemes, not all of them sober, were put forward to avoid the horror of a Labour government. A succession of stop-gap Prime Ministers was proposed including Balfour, Neville Chamberlain, his half-brother Austen, Asquith, and even Reginald McKenna as the head of a government of National Trustees!

Baldwin's position was clear. He stated that he had 'killed one coalition and would never join another' (i.e., with the Liberals against Labour); he considered that Labour must be asked to form an administration. Asquith, who had once more superseded Lloyd George as chief Liberal counsellor, also believed that MacDonald must be sent for. Maybe both Baldwin and Asquith were acting from the highest motives; maybe both expected to succeed to power on the speedy collapse of Labour. In any event, King George took their advice, which accorded with his own opinion that Labour must be given a fair chance. When Parliament met in January 1924, the Conservatives were defeated in the Commons by seventy-two votes, and Baldwin resigned.

The King then sent for Ramsay MacDonald, determined to accord him 'the same facilities which would be accorded to any Minister entrusted by the Sovereign with the formation of a Government'. He later wrote that 'I never consulted Mr Baldwin in any way when he came to resign, nor asked his advice as to whom to send for.' But, then, the King already knew what Baldwin's advice would have been. On 22 January, MacDonald was sworn in as a Privy Councillor and asked to form an administration. King George's own words, plain but touched with a sense of wonder, are a sufficient description of this momentous interview:

> At 12.15 I held a Council, at which Mr Ramsay MacDonald was sworn as a member. I then asked him to form a Government, which he accepted to do. I had an hour's talk with him, he impressed me very much; he wishes to do the right thing.
>
> Today 23 years ago dear Grandmama died. I wonder what she would have thought of a Labour Government!

OPPOSITE
Ramsay MacDonald arriving at Number 10 Downing Street for the first Cabinet meeting of the new government in January 1924.

7 Storms, Calms and 1924-31

Uncertain Courses

Ramsay macdonald's first Labour government was more anxious to prove its respectability and administrative competence than to plunge the nation into a socialist revolution. In any case, it relied upon the Liberals for support in the House of Commons and had no wish to alienate them. The Cabinet was a nice balance between trade unionists and the predominantly middle-class members of E. D. Morel's Union of Democratic Control. Working men and intellectuals rubbed shoulders in the Cabinet room: J. H. Thomas, the railwaymen's leader (who had once predicted that the first Labour Prime Minister would either be 'me or 'Enderson') with C. P. Trevelyan; J. R. Clynes, the ex-mill hand, with Sidney Webb. The most committed socialist was John Wheatley, a Roman Catholic from the 'red' Clydeside; a more prominent member of the Labour left wing, George Lansbury, was left out, at least partly because the King had objected to his reminder during the political hiatus immediately after the recent election that 'Some centuries ago a King stood against the common people and he lost his head.'

No member of the Cabinet, however, was eager to play Oliver Cromwell to King George's Charles I. From Mac-Donald to the most junior minister they strove to make themselves agreeable; those who needed to, hired Court dress – a sensible concession in view of the King's almost obsessional concern with such formalities. The new Prime Minister, when challenged by the monarch on the singing of the *Red Flag* and the *Marseillaise* at a recent meeting in the Albert Hall, replied:

> he was sure the King would be generous to him and understand the very difficult position he was in *vis-a-vis* his own extremists.... Moreover there was a serious possibility on Monday night of the *Red Flag* being sung in the House of Commons and it required all his influence ... to prevent this taking place: they had got into the way of singing this song and it will be by degrees that he hopes to break down this habit.

PREVIOUS PAGES
Armoured cars and troops assemble at Hyde Park Corner before escorting the food convoy from the London docks during the General Strike.

The King was impressed by Ramsay MacDonald's considerate behaviour and by his fine bearing. He took pains to become personally acquainted with all his new ministers and was soon able to tell his mother, Queen Alexandra, 'I must say they all seem to be very intelligent & they take things very seriously. They have different ideas to ours as they are all socialists, but

174

they ought to be given a chance & ought to be treated fairly.'

In fact, the government was given only a short lease of ten months before forced to fight, and lose, another General Election. In domestic matters Labour could not hope to achieve much. They lacked an overall majority and thus a mandate to mount an effective assault on the capitalist system. The Clydesider, Wheatley, was one of the few ministers to effect any real

Labour leaders in 1924. Left to right: Ramsay MacDonald, J.H. Thomas, Arthur Henderson, J. R. Clynes.

175

OUTSIDE THE HOUSE OF COMMONS.

"'ERE Y'ARE, SIR—WORDS AND MUSIC, 'THE RED FLAG.'"

change when his Housing Act secured an expansion of the building industry, increased the housing subsidy by fifty per cent, and ensured that councils would provide only accommodation to rent. In education, Trevelyan set up the Hadow Committee which eventually reported in favour of raising the school-leaving age to fifteen and creating a break at eleven years to distinguish between primary and secondary schooling.

Other sweeping reforms were not attempted. Perhaps more important than the government's desire to be moderate and to survive was the problem of financing an ambitious reforming programme. The Chancellor, Philip Snowden, wanted to balance the budget, not go down in history as a Treasury spend-thrift. Snowden's caution, and indeed that of the administration generally, meant that social reform had to be pushed aside, or rather to some time ahead, when more favourable conditions would prevail. The government also failed to relieve the plight of the million or so unemployed, perhaps chiefly because there was no apparent remedy. Nor did the advent of a Labour administration usher in an era of tranquillity on the industrial relations front; engine-drivers, dockers and London tram-workers went ahead with strike action, and the Cabinet prepared to use the Emergency Powers Act which they had earlier denounced while in opposition.

Ramsay MacDonald had taken the Foreign Office in addition to the premiership, and against the King's advice that the joint burden might prove unbearable. Yet it was in this area that Labour could hope to effect most change; the restraining hand of the Chancellor could be shrugged off in diplomatic forays and international initiatives. MacDonald intervened first in the reparations dispute, and skilfully persuaded France to accept the Dawes Committee's plan to allow Germany to pay sums within her capacity to the Allies. Franco-German relations were thus to some extent desensitised. The Prime Minister also sought to foster the League of Nations, and took the unprecedented step of attending its sessions. He hoped, through the Geneva Protocol, to provide an effective international guarantee of existing European frontiers, particularly those between France and Germany. The fact that the Labour government, before it fell, was unable to ratify the Protocol, and that the incoming Conservatives chose not to, did not wholly destroy

A contemporary *Punch* cartoon on the first Labour government. Ramsay MacDonald told the King he hoped 'by degrees to break down' the party's habit of singing the *Red Flag*.

MacDonald's achievement. It was enough that he had utilised the League of Nations on the one hand, and concentrated on reducing Franco-German anxieties and resentments on the other.

Labour's decision to recognise Soviet Russia was a less successful innovation in foreign policy. Despite Conservative and Liberal detestation of 'Bolshevism', there was much to be said for establishing normal diplomatic relations with Russia; one practical consideration being that there could then be a reasonable settlement of the pre-revolutionary debts owed to Britain. The King had no love for the Bolsheviks, and had early on quibbled with MacDonald over the exact nature of Soviet representation, pointing out 'how abhorrent it would be to His Majesty to receive any representative of Russia who, directly or indirectly, had been connected with the abominable murder of the Emperor, Empress and their family, the King's own first cousin'.

It was not, however, King George's lingering sense of outrage, nor the anti-Bolshevik convictions of Conservatives which provided the major stumbling-block to MacDonald's attempt at improving Anglo-Soviet relations. The Russian government itself created a furore when it asked for a loan in exchange for a part-settlement of outstanding debts. After some negotiations, in which left-wing Labour MPs played a significant part, a compromise was reached regarding the loan. But both the Conservative and Liberal opposition parties denounced the prospect of a loan to Soviet Russia, and when the Parliamentary summer recess began in August 1924, there was much public criticism of Labour's recent performance.

The Communist bogy did not melt away with the warmth of summer, and the Campbell case further troubled the government. J.R. Campbell, the editor of a Communist journal *The Worker's Weekly*, was accused of sedition for urging soldiers not to shoot at strikers if ordered to do so. Such appeals from the extreme left were not uncommon, and had occasionally come from within the ranks of the Labour movement. It is not clear why Campbell came to the brink of prosecution; perhaps, as the Prime Minister later explained to the King, there had been 'a muddle somewhere'. At any rate, MacDonald ordered the Attorney General to drop the prosecution. He thus fell uncomfortably between two stools: the government had allowed proceedings to begin, and then had backed down – apparently because of left-wing Labour pressure. The opposition could argue that perhaps the old and untidy equation between Labour and the Communists had some truth in it after all. Legal purists could complain that there had been political tampering with the course of justice. When Parliament reassembled in September 1924, a vote of censure on the government was debated. Asquith's compromise proposal of a select committee of enquiry was voted down by the Conservatives and all but fourteen of the Liberals. MacDonald then asked the King for an immediate dissolution of Parliament.

King George was once more faced with a constitutional situation without precedent, since the request for a dissolution came from a Prime Minister who did not possess a majority in the Commons. It was only after he had consulted with Baldwin and Asquith, and discovered that they could not form alternative administrations, that he granted MacDonald a dissolution, though 'regretting the necessity for doing so, being aware how strongly the country at large deprecates another General Election within less than a year'. Polling took place on 29 October, three weeks after the dissolution. The election campaign was marked by the sensation of the 'Zinoviev letter'. This letter, urging the British Communist party to foment mutiny and sedition, was allegedly the work of Zinoviev, President of the Third International. The King doubted the authenticity of the letter, but its contents were published and seemed, in some roundabout way, to confirm suspicions that the Labour party was soft on Communism.

The election results of October 1924 swept the Conservatives back to power with an overall majority in the Commons. The Liberals lost over one hundred seats. Though Labour had a net loss of forty seats, their vote increased by over a million – hardly a sign that the Zinoviev letter had done them irreparable harm. Former Liberal voters swung over to the Conservatives, perhaps chiefly because Baldwin had repudiated economic protection. The significant feature of the election was arguably not the triumph of the Conservatives, but the decline of the Liberals, who were now reduced to a Parliamentary rump of forty members. Labour was the main opposition party, with ten more seats than after the 1922 election. Thus King George, advised by Baldwin and Asquith, had helped to entrench the Labour party's position by sending for MacDonald in January 1924. Increasingly, the electorate saw their political choice as lying between the Conservatives and Labour; the Liberals were squeezed out as serious contenders for power. In a sense, therefore, the King can be seen as the foster father of a really effective Labour party, a role which would have brought him little joy in his earlier years.

Baldwin's second administration lasted from 1924–29. It contained powerful figures like Curzon, Austen and Neville Chamberlain, Lord Birkenhead, and a recanted Winston Churchill, in the not altogether appropriate office of Chancellor of the Exchequer. Baldwin's instinct was to play down the contentious issues of the interwar years: the class war, free trade versus protection, industrial conflict. Even when his government had to cope with the general strike of 1926, he adopted a neo-Asquithian policy of 'wait and see'. When the Dominion Prime Ministers assembled later in 1926 for what promised to be the stormiest Imperial Conference for decades, Baldwin's chief contribution (according to his Colonial Secretary, Leopold Amery) was to puff his pipe and, like Brer Rabbit, 'lie low and say nuffin''.

The general strike (or, more correctly, the national strike) grew out of a protracted crisis in the coal industry. By 1925, foreign competition had undercut the price of British coal in the European market, and the coal mines began to run at a loss. British mine-owners proposed the classical, Victorian remedy of reduced wages and longer hours. A.J. Cook, the miners' secretary, was a former Baptist lay preacher and, in his words, 'a humble follower of Lenin'. His impassioned advice to the miners to stand firm was, in principle, no different from that of their president, Herbert Smith, who said to the owners 'Nowt doing.' The government intervened in the crisis and patched up a truce while a Royal Commission investigated the working of the coal industry. The King had contemplated the prospect of a coal strike with gloom and a little self-pity, writing on 29 July, 'I fear a strike now is inevitable at the end of the week. It will play the devil in the country. I never seem to get any peace in

Stanley Baldwin
at Chequers in
November 1924.

this world. Feel very low and depressed.' He was at least given
a nine months' respite from anxiety before the Royal Commission reported in March 1926.

The three-hundred-page report offered some long-term
improvements in the organisation and conditions of work in the
industry; but it also recommended an immediate reduction of
wages. The miners echoed Cook's reply, 'Not a penny off the

City workers in Leyton boarding one of the many lorries used as emergency transport during the General Strike.

pay, not a minute on the day.' The mine-owners insisted on both concessions, thus giving weight to Lord Birkenhead's previous judgment that 'I should call them [the miners] the stupidest men in England if I had not previously had to deal with the owners.' After a month of wrangling, the miners were locked-out, appropriately enough on 1 May. The General Council of the TUC approved plans for a national strike to begin on 3 May. Last minute attempts to divert both sides from their collision course failed, and at midnight on 3 May the big unions, the transport workers, railwaymen, workers in building and heavy industry, and in gas and electricity, came out; so did the printers. Smaller unions were kept in reserve, while the big ones went 'over the top'; still eighty per cent of the trade union movement was involved.

The general strike caused much bitterness, but not the bloody class warfare many had feared. Although one minister, Winston Churchill, relished the situation and attempted to provoke conflict by describing strikers as 'the enemy' and by using armoured cars to escort supplies through the streets, the Prime Minister had no such inclinations. King George, who considered the strikers to be just as much his subjects as merchant-bankers and newspaper-proprietors, strongly advised the government against introducing emergency measures which would have deprived the unions of funds, arguing that it would be 'a grave mistake to do anything which might be interpreted as confiscation, or to provoke the strikers, who until now have been remarkably quiet'.

The King perhaps exaggerated the extent of tranquillity, since there was some violence in the mining areas, Glasgow and the working-class districts and docklands of London; a number of strike-breaking buses were attacked, and in Durham there was an attempt to sabotage a train; eventually, more than three thousand people were charged with acts of violence, or with seeking to incite such acts. But considering that there were over four million strikers, the rarity of these incidents indicates either remarkable self-discipline or indifference, perhaps a mixture of both. Broadly speaking, however, the middle classes confronted the working classes during these tense days; at one extreme, ex-officers and undergraduates enrolled as special constables, like their forebears during the Chartist disturbances in 1848; on the other, syndicalists and Communists talked of revolution. Probably all that the vast numbers in-between wanted was a reasonable compromise.

In the interests of compromise, and convinced that the government were in no mood to surrender, the TUC called off the general strike unconditionally after nine days. The King greeted the news thankfully: 'It is indeed a great relief to me as I have been very anxious about the situation. Our old country can well be proud of itself as during the last nine days there has been a strike in which 4 million men have been affected; not a shot has been fired & no one killed; it shows what a wonderful people we are.' But the miners had no cause for celebration; they continued their strike for six months until near-starvation drove them back to the pits. They lost on all counts: their wages were cut, their hours increased, their conditions of work were

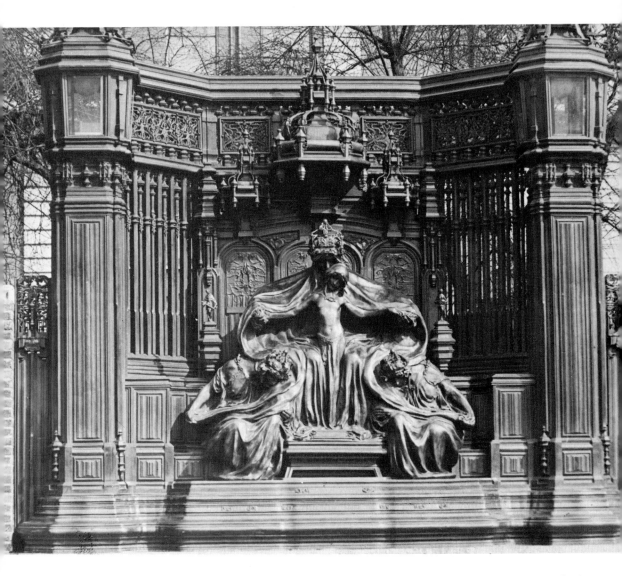

The memorial to Queen Alexandra set in the wall of Marlborough House, where she lived after the death of Edward VII.

not improved. The trade union movement, as a whole, escaped similar treatment, though in 1927 the Conservatives brought in an amended Trade Disputes Act, which declared any sympathetic strike aimed at coercing the government to be illegal. This act was never invoked, and was repealed after Labour's crushing election victory in 1945. Still, it provided part of the uncomfortable legacy of the unions' defeat in 1926.

The government could claim two other notable achievements, apart from beating the general strike, by the end of 1926. One was the signing of the Locarno Treaty, and the other was the agreement reached at the Imperial Conference. Neither area of activity was particularly controversial, and while the nation could generally endorse the Locarno Treaty, a detailed account of the achievements of the Imperial Conference would probably have sent most citizens to sleep. The agreement signed at Locarno was a non-aggression pact between France, Germany and Belgium, which was guaranteed by Britain and Italy. Its spirit owed much to MacDonald's earlier initiatives, and the treaty was generally greeted as the dawn of a new era in European relations. In fact, there was no reasonably effective way in which Britain, let alone Italy, could guarantee the boundaries between France, Belgium and Germany; perhaps the will to intervene was absent too.

The Imperial Conference of 1926 redefined the constitutional status of the Dominions to the satisfaction of even South Africa and the Irish Free State. Lord Balfour and General Hertzog, the Nationalist Prime Minister of South Africa, between them produced a definition of Dominion status which, despite its verbal convolutions and obscurities, was hailed as a masterpiece of constructive statesmanship. In this way the self-governing Commonwealth probably got the definition it deserved. Other areas of dispute between Britain and the Dominions, such as the exact role of the Governors-General, the application to the Dominions of treaties signed by Britain with foreign powers, and the theoretical though trifling restrictions imposed on Dominion autonomy by the British Crown and Parliament, were all cleared up. The King, who had for so long cherished the hope that he would see closer bonds forged between Britain and the Dominions, thus saw the more anachronistic links severed, and the results of the Conferences of 1926 and 1930 put before Parliament and passed in his name as the Statute of Westminster in 1931.

The period 1924–31 troubled King George in more personal ways. In November 1925, his mother died, just before her eighty-first birthday. Queen Alexandra had outlived her husband by fifteen years and, despite her deafness and her increasingly poor memory, had remained a vital and irreplaceable member of the royal family. Ever since his brother Eddy's death in 1892, King George had been the only son of a devoted and apparently ageless mother; he could no longer enjoy this privilege. The year 1931 brought other losses: in January, that of the King's eldest sister the Princess Royal; two week's later, his oldest friend and equerry Sir Charles Cust died; in March, the King's Private Secretary, Lord Stamfordham, upon whom he had relied so heavily for advice and encouragement, also died; finally, in July, the King learned of the death of his old tutor, Canon Dalton, who had first taken charge of his education sixty years before.

These deaths severed some of the King's most important links with what he considered to be a golden and naturally unrepeatable past – the time of his childhood and young manhood. In part, this may explain his increasing impatience with modern trends, with new fashions and manners, with the hectic pace of life in the 1920s, and with vehement criticism of old ways and entrenched standards. King George had always valued his domestic routine, and it now became more difficult than ever to disturb it. Fortunately, Queen Mary was prepared to forego theatre trips and attendances at social functions, and, as far as possible, tried to ensure that a shield of quiet privacy came between the King and some of the contemporary phenomena he found so irritating.

The King's health had also begun to fail. In February 1925, he developed severe bronchitis after a bout of influenza. Grudgingly, he agreed to a restorative Mediterranean cruise. It was not altogether a success, for though his health improved, he and his sister Princess Victoria had no inclination to examine Sicilian antiquities or marvel at the ruins of Pompeii. As a result, 'The King is bored, as one would expect. The Queen angry because nobody else cares to sight-see; and Princess Victoria very restless & no sooner begins one thing than she wants to do another.' This unhappy experience, coupled with a somewhat insular outlook, doubtless accounts for King George's adamant refusal to undertake similar trips to Europe for the sake of his health.

In the late autumn of 1928, however, the King suffered an almost fatal setback. In November, he developed a dangerous illness as a result of a pleural abscess, awkwardly situated behind the diaphragm, and exceedingly difficult to find and drain. His heart began to fail, the Prince of Wales returned post-haste from East Africa, and a Council of State was formed. At the end of three weeks, the King was unconscious for much of the time, and there seemed no prospect of recovery. Fortunately, his physician, Lord Dawson, finally located the abscess and within hours carried out an operation.

The King began to recover slowly, though it was three months before he was able to grant an audience to the Prime Minister. Even so, he suffered two relapses; one in May 1929 when a second operation was performed to remove a new abscess, and the other in July, which necessitated a further operation. The second relapse was apparently brought on by a visit from J. H. Thomas, the ex-railwaymen's leader, who had just become Lord Privy Seal in the second Labour government. The King always found Jimmy Thomas the most congenial of company, and valued the straightforward and unpretentious relationship which existed between them. Thomas, was, for example, able to explain that the reason why the younger members of the royal family did not much care to go to Balmoral was because it was 'such a bloody dull 'ouse'. He also kept the King supplied with stories of a boisterous and frequently risqué character, and it was as a result of immoderate laughter at one of Thomas's jokes that the King suffered his second relapse. This is perhaps the nearest that a senior member of the Labour party has ever come to killing the monarch, and then only through kindness.

King George's protracted illness and difficult convalescence imposed a considerable strain upon his constitution. Although he had six more years to live, his health remained variable. Like his father before him, he was not a good patient, and became easily bored. He could be diverted by film shows, however, and he found particular pleasure in the company of his grandchildren, especially Princess Elizabeth, the future Queen Elizabeth II. Indeed, in March 1929, Princess Elizabeth, then nearly three years old, came to stay at Bognor accompanied by her nurse. The arrival of his favourite grandchild did much to lift King George's spirits, and Queen Mary's diary recorded 'G. delighted to see her.' The King's diary, too, reveals the enormous pleasure he gained from Princess Elizabeth's companionship.

By May, King George and Queen Mary were able to return to Windsor. A grave illness had been surmounted. Throughout,

David Low's cartoon of J. H. Thomas whose jokes made the convalescent King laugh so much that he suffered a relapse.

OPPOSITE The King and Queen with Princess Elizabeth at Bognor while the King was convalescing from his illness.

the Queen had coped so stoically with her private fears that she had prompted her second son, the Duke of York, to remark to the Prince of Wales, 'Through all the anxiety she has never once revealed her feelings to any of us. She is really far too reserved; she keeps too much locked up inside herself.' But the nation at large had clearly shown how much it cared for the King's recovery. This affection was manifested in the eager rush to read bulletins reporting his progress, in the lonely vigils of individuals, in the widespread offering of prayers and in the £689,597 subscribed to the Thanksgiving Fund for his recovery. The extent of his people's regard was to be more formally manifested during the Silver Jubilee celebrations in 1935, but it was expressed spontaneously and whole-heartedly throughout the winter of 1928–29.

While the King was still convalescing, a General Election was fought in May 1929, when the Parliament elected in 1924 had almost run its statutory term. The election was a genuine three-cornered fight between the major parties; each ran some five hundred candidates; each had a distinctive platform; each could boast a leader of proven ability in Baldwin, MacDonald and Lloyd George. They did not, however, receive identical treatment at the hands of the electorate, which included for the first time women aged between twenty-one and thirty-five years – the 'flapper vote'. The Conservatives and Labour each polled more than eight million votes, the Liberals five million. But Labour won 288 seats, the Conservatives 260, and the Liberals 49. Instead of facing the House of Commons, as he had done in 1924, Baldwin took the view that the voice of the people must be heeded, and resigned immediately; this course at least denied Lloyd George, as leader of the Liberal MPs, any opportunity of making or unmaking the Prime Minister.

On 5 June, the King received Ramsay MacDonald in his bedroom at Windsor and invited him to form an administration. Although recovering from his first relapse, the King showed a keen interest in the formation of the new government. Mac-Donald had agreed not to take the Foreign Office again, though apparently only after contemplating handing the premiership to a senior colleague in order to concentrate on the Foreign Secretaryship himself. The King suggested J. H. Thomas for the Foreign Office at the meeting on 5 June, but the post was

A carload of flappers with
Captain Ian Fraser arriving
at the polling station in
May 1929 to vote. This
was the first time in
British history that women
under thirty-five had been
allowed to vote in
Parliamentary elections.

eventually given to Arthur Henderson. The second Labour government included the first woman Cabinet minister, Margaret Bondfield; it was also dominated by those on the right of the party; one exception was George Lansbury, who became First Commissioner of Works, and who managed to get on well with the King (whose head he had once seemed to demand), by encouraging a mutual interest in each other's illnesses.

The Labour government lasted from June 1929 to August 1931. Once more lacking an overall majority, much of its domestic legislation was crippled; it failed to repeal the 1927 Trade Disputes Act, Trevelyan's Education Bill was defeated in the Lords, and an attempt at electoral reform perished. As in 1924, its main achievements were outside the United Kingdom: MacDonald had reserved Anglo-American relations for his own delicate diplomatic touch, and in 1930 had lured the United States into signing the London Naval Treaty which limited the naval building programmes of the leading maritime powers; in India, Labour strove for the conciliation of the Congress movement, and eventually got Gandhi's agreement to attend a Round Table Conference in London, though this did not take place while the government held office; in the Middle East, Arthur Henderson tried to negotiate with the Egyptian government a treaty which, while preserving essential British interest in the Suez route, would also satisfy Egyptian nationalist feeling.

These diplomatic initiatives were played out against the sombre background of the Great Depression, which had settled over the world in October 1929. The collapse of American credit damaged all those nations who had relied upon the steady flow of United States' loans and investments. World markets shrank, and millions were thrown out of work. By December 1930, Britain had two and a half million unemployed; a year later, the figure was nearer three million. The dole queue was no new experience for the British public, but this time the experience had a wider and more humiliating application.

What could be done? MacDonald fell back on the traditional recipe of blaming the capitalist system; J. H. Thomas, who was the Minister responsible for coping with unemployment, had no effective remedies; Conservatives opposed raising income tax, Labour detested talk of 'economy measures'; few men understood the new economic theories of Maynard Keynes, and those who did were in no position to force them upon the nation. One of the more obviously talented of the junior Labour ministers, Sir Oswald Mosley, believed he could see the way through, but was thwarted in his advocacy, and left office to form his New Party; this was an ill-fated enterprise, and eventually Mosley was transformed from one of Labour's young eagles into one of international Fascism's lame ducks.

By the summer of 1931, a visible trade gap and a budget deficit helped to cause a disastrous run on sterling. Something like panic seized the City and various panaceas were touted; a majority of MacDonald's Cabinet colleagues, however, refused to accept the proposal to cut unemployment benefits in order to propitiate foreign bankers. But the resignation of the whole Cabinet, followed by an almost punitive attack on the unemployed, was too risky for the Conservative and Liberal leadership to contemplate singlehanded. Sir Herbert Samuel, deputising for the indisposed Lloyd George, proposed to the King that MacDonald should head a National government, supported by all three parties. In the late evening of 23 August 1931, the Prime Minister left an impassioned Cabinet meeting apparently intent on resigning. He reached Buckingham Palace looking 'scared and unbalanced', according to one account, and offered his Cabinet's resignation. The King, who held MacDonald's more positive qualities in high esteem, argued that 'he was the only man to lead the country through the crisis' and hoped that 'he would reconsider the situation'. MacDonald responded to this appeal. No doubt he wished also to be the saviour of his country, even at the expense of temporarily ruining his party. At any rate, on 24 August he was sworn in as the leader of a National Government.

'The only man to lead the country through the crisis'

ABOVE George V
by Calkin.

OPPOSITE George V on his favourite
horse, Kildare, by George Scott.

8
Towards the Jubilee
1931-6

IN ACCEPTING THE KING'S invitation to form a National Government, Ramsay MacDonald destroyed his standing in the Labour party. Of the Cabinet, the Prime Minister was able to persuade only J. H. Thomas, Lord Sankey and, with some difficulty, his Chancellor, Philip Snowden, to join him in the new administration. He also told the Labour junior ministers that if they followed him they were risking their political futures; all but four took his advice and disassociated themselves. On 28 August, the Parliamentary party elected Arthur Henderson leader in MacDonald's place. Three days later, the Hampstead Labour party expelled MacDonald from their local membership, and the executive committee of the National Union of Railwaymen accepted J. H. Thomas's resignation as political secretary. When the Prime Minister next faced the House of Commons, in September, all but a handful of his former Cabinet colleagues and supporters were ranged against him on the opposition benches. Amid a storm of attack and counter-attack, the Labour movement painfully reassessed MacDonald, eventually producing a murky picture of class-betrayal and self-seeking that has obstinately survived the passage of forty-odd years.

The Prime Minister may have drawn some comfort from a warm, but over-optimistic, letter from the King who wrote 'I should like to assure you how much I appreciate & admire the courage with which you have put aside all personal & party interest in order to stand by the country in this grave national crisis. By this proof of strength of character & devotion to duty your name will always hold an honoured place among British Statesmen.' Rank and file Labour MPs did not entertain such a flattering view; instead they saw their erstwhile leader surrounded by Conservative and Liberal ministers, aided and abetted by a few turncoat Labour men.

There was much else that was galling for Labour. Between August and October 1931 the National Government cut all salaries paid by the state, including unemployment benefit, by ten per cent; these economies were rewarded by a loan of £80,000,000 from foreign bankers; when the run on sterling continued, the government suspended the gold standard, and accepted an effective twenty-five per cent devaluation of the pound, which helped British exports. The immediate crisis

PREVIOUS PAGES The King and Queen with Princess Elizabeth driving from Crathie Church in 1932.

198

seemed over, and the General Election results in October reflected both relief and disillusion with the turn of events. The Conservatives, with their allies the 'National' Liberals and the 'National' Labour men (followers of MacDonald), polled a record sixty per cent of the vote and won 521 seats. The Labour vote shrank by almost two million, though massive abstentions rather than a switch of allegiance explains this slump. There were only fifty-six Labour MPs in the new House of Commons, scarcely more than in 1906, but at least unsullied by political compromise and hopeful that, one day, the electoral pendulum would swing back to them.

King George was most anxious that the National Government should succeed in establishing itself as a stable administration capable of riding out the economic crisis, but the period between the fall of the Labour government and the election of October 1931 was notable for its uncertainties. The King was impatient with Lloyd George's erratic political behaviour, and

Posters for the General Election of 1931 reflected the fears of industrial depression and the need to appeal to women as voters.

199

with Sir Herbert Samuel's refusal to compromise the Liberal party's espousal of free trade. Ramsay MacDonald was also beset with doubts, and at the beginning of October talked of resignation. The King's response was some brisk and salty advice to 'brace himself up to realise that he was the only person to tackle the present chaotic state of affairs'. Moreover, it was made plain that the King would not accept the Prime Minister's resignation even if it was offered.

MacDonald soldiered on as Prime Minister until 1935. His lot was not a happy one. The Labour opposition regarded him as a pariah; the Conservative backbone of the National Government were prepared merely to tolerate him. When Sir Herbert Samuel, Sir Archibald Sinclair and Lord Snowden resigned from the Cabinet in 1932, MacDonald expressed his anguish at these defections in a letter to the King, in which he said 'I think Your Majesty will find that a Prime Minister who does not belong to the Party in power will become more and more an anomaly, and, as policy develops, his position will become more and more degrading.' Events were to prove the accuracy of Ramsay MacDonald's mournful diagnosis. Although he remained Prime Minister until the autumn of 1935, his reputation was rendered even more threadbare by the obvious blurring of his mental faculties. His fine oratorical displays became a shambles, his powers of concentration declined to an embarrassing extent. Baldwin took over at 10 Downing Street; at last the 'family doctor' had inherited the 'doctor's mandate' of the 1931 General Election.

'A Prime Minister who does not belong to the Party in power will become more and more an anomaly'

Whether the British body politic needed sedation or a dose of stimulants in 1935 was not clear. The years since the formation of the National Government had seen some progress on the domestic front, and the advent of alarming phenomena abroad. At home, the number of unemployed fell steadily during 1933; world trade as a whole began to pick up; the extension of British tariffs did something to expand inter-imperial commerce. Generally, wages remained stable, and prices fell. Increased domestic consumption helped to encourage domestic economic recovery; new industries sprang up and a housing boom developed. British exports, however, continued to be a source of disappointment.

Within the Empire, Indian nationalism had achieved

200

substantial progress with the 1935 Government of India Act. This Act set up responsible government in the eleven provinces of British India, and made provision for the establishment of a central federal government if a certain number of the princely states were willing to join in such a federation. King George had long nurtured the hope that India could be kept within the Empire, pacified, to some extent reformed, and loyal to the King-Emperor. He had opposed the Morley-Minto reforms of 1908–9, and had looked askance at subsequent concessions to Indian nationalism. But, like so many others of conservative outlook, he was forced to adjust his views to the remarkable success of Gandhi's non-co-operation movement. In 1931; he met Gandhi when the latter attended the Second Round Table Conference in London. According to Sir Clive Wigram, who had succeeded Lord Stamfordham as Private Secretary in 1931, the King was 'as is his custom, very nice to [Mr Gandhi], but ended up by impressing on him that this country would not stand a campaign of terrorism and having their friends shot down in India. His Majesty warned Gandhi that he was to put a stop to this.... Gandhi spluttered some excuse, but H.M. said he held him responsible.'

Gandhi's splutterings were more than justified. The ascetic Congress leader had set his face sternly against violence, and to hold him responsible for various outrages was to misunderstand the rationale of his campaign. But the King had even harder words for the Indian princes when they refused to co-operate in forming a wider federation under the 1935 Government of India Act. King George had put much faith in the stabilising and conservative influence of the Indian princes; he now told the India Office that he was 'disgusted by their vacillation', and that they would do better to stay at home caring for their subjects than coming to Britain for the 1935 Jubilee celebrations.

Events in Europe were meanwhile being shaped by forces far more dynamic than Indian nationalism, and of measureless malignancy. The rise of European Fascism, and the chauvinistic belligerence of Japan in the Far East, were portents of a terrible conflict. Not that these dangers were immediately and universally evident to contemporary opinion. Mussolini had been in power in Italy since 1922 and, despite his ultra-nationalist

Hitler at a party rally at
Bückeberg in 1934.

posturing, had been willing to work with other European governments through the normal apparatus of diplomacy. Hitler had attained the German Chancellorship in 1933 through more or less democratic means, and seemed to many in the West to provide a sure shield against the alleged Bolshevik menace from the East.

In any case, the governments of the leading powers were not apparently bent on war; rearmament was not a popular cause with the electorate, and those who demanded it, like Winston Churchill, seemed at variance with their fellows. If any country should threaten the peace, then theoretically the League of Nations could intervene. Of course, there were clear signs that international harmony could not be taken for granted: in 1931 Japan seized Manchuria, and the League's rebukes led to a Japanese withdrawal from the organisation; in 1933, Nazi Germany also left the League after the Disarmament Conference, which first met in 1932, failed to satisfy Hitler's demand for military parity with France; in 1935, Italian armies invaded the backward, but still independent, African kingdom of Abyssinia.

King George reacted to these developments with his characteristic honesty and with considerable insight. In 1934, he treated the German ambassador to some plain speaking, telling him that 'at the present moment Germany was the peril of the world, and that, if she went on at her present rate, there was bound to be a war within ten years... what was Germany arming for?' The ambassador pointed out that the French fortifications, along the Maginot line, were impregnable, and that Germany had no fortifications on her side. The King dismissed this argument, and said that 'in the last war fortifications were useless and would be even more so in the next'. He was later sharply critical of Germany's attempts to create a rift between Britain and France, and rejected Hitler's suggestion in a letter written to the press baron Lord Rothermere in 1935 that Anglo-German co-operation would ensure world peace. 'The French,' King George remarked, 'are not mentioned in the letter from start to finish and it seems to me, reading between the lines, that Hitler's object is to form a block against the French and other countries in Europe, which is entirely contrary to our present Foreign Policy.'

The lengthening shadows of the Nazis' crooked cross could not, however, dim the celebration of the twenty-fifth anniversary of King George's accession to the throne. To the Golden and Diamond Jubilees of Queen Victoria's reign was now added the Silver Jubilee of 1935. On 6 May, the King and Queen drove to St Paul's Cathedral for a service of thanksgiving. The King wrote in his diary that it was 'A never to be forgotten day, when we celebrated our Silver Jubilee. It was a glorious summer's day: 75° in the shade. The greatest number of people in the streets that I have ever seen. The enthusiasm was most touching.'

For nearly a month, the King and Queen were the object of loyal official addresses and of the warm and spontaneous greetings of the people of London. Throughout the country, flags and bunting adorned a multitude of public and private buildings and Jubilee tea-parties were held outside for the children. Sometimes the royal couple undertook unheralded car trips to the London suburbs where, on one occasion, Queen Mary noted 'the decorations in the smaller streets... were very touching, many people recognized us and cheered'. The King was equally moved by a particularly exhausting but rapturous reception in the East End, and remarked with his habitual candour 'I'd no idea they felt like that about me. I am beginning to think they must like me for myself.'

'I am beginning to think they must like me for myself'

It would be easy enough to dismiss these manifestations of public enthusiasm as a predictable response to a month of bread and circuses. But contemporary observers felt that there was more to it than that. King George had clearly established an enviable rapport with his people which owed nothing to artifice or deep calculation. The British public were responding to the unpretentious, trustworthy, ordinary man who was their monarch, and whose reassuring and unadorned voice spoke to them on the night of 6 May over the radio, as on the three previous Christmas Days:

> At the close of this memorable day, I must speak to my people everywhere. How can I express what is in my heart? ... I can only say to you, my very, very dear people, that the Queen and I thank you from the depths of our hearts for all the loyalty – and may I say so? – the love, with which this day and always you have surrounded us. I dedicate myself anew to your service for all the years that may still be given me.

The Royal Family entering
the west door of
St Paul's Cathedral for the
Jubilee Service of Thanksgiving.
Behind the King stand the Lord
Chamberlain, the Prince of Wales
and the Duke and Duchess of York,
with Princess Elizabeth and
Princess Margaret. The Duke
of Gloucester is to the right
of the Duke of York and the
Duke of Kent stands behind on
the left. Stanley Baldwin is at the
side of Queen Mary and the
Indian Princes bring up the tail of
the procession. The painting,
entitled 'O Enter then His Gates
with Praise', hangs in the Guildhall.

ABOVE The Royal
Family on the balcony of
Buckingham Palace during
the Silver Jubilee.
Balcony appearances first
became traditional in
George V's reign when the
balcony was added to the
front of the palace as
part of the refacing design.

RIGHT Jubilee celebrations
and decorations in Dudley
Street, Paddington.

ABOVE The procession to St Paul's for the thanksgiving service rounds Hyde Park Corner.

209

ABOVE George V at the microphone. King George
was the first British King to use the radio
as a means of reaching vast numbers of his people.

OPPOSITE The King in
his last years.

In fact, the King had only seven months to live. Early in November 1935, the family celebrated the wedding of Prince Henry, Duke of Gloucester to Lady Alice Scott, and Queen Mary recorded that two of the bridesmaids (the Princesses Elizabeth and Margaret) 'looked too sweet'. But a few days later, the King was not well enough to attend the annual remembrance service at the Cenotaph. On 3 December, he was grief-stricken to learn that his favourite sister, Victoria, had died, and cancelled the state opening of Parliament scheduled for that afternoon. He never appeared in public again.

The Christmas festivities at Sandringham were thus overhung with a sense of impending doom. Although King George delivered his Christmas Day radio broadcast to his people, he felt ill and weak, and quite unable to indulge his life-long passion for shooting on the Sandringham estate. During the first days of the New Year, he managed to go for rides upon Jock, his white pony, but on 17 January 1936, he wrote in his diary for the last time, 'A little snow & wind. Dawson [his chief physician] arrived. I saw him and feel rotten.' The Prince of Wales, who was shooting at Windsor, was summoned to Sandringham by Queen Mary. He arrived by aeroplane; it was a symbolic contrast between the life-styles of the dying monarch and the heir to the throne.

On 19 January, the Prince of Wales motored to London to inform the Prime Minister, Baldwin, that the King was dying. During these last few momentous days, King George sat in front of a bright fire in his bedroom at Sandringham, wearing a Tibetan dressing-gown he had brought back from one of his visits to his beloved India. The nation listened for the medical bulletins issued by the BBC, and eventually heard that 'The King's life is moving peacefully to its close'. On 20 January, King George died tranquilly in the presence of his wife and children, and after struggling, with his usual sense of duty, to sign the proclamation setting up a Council of State. Queen Mary wrote in her diary '*Am heartbroken*... at 5 to 12 my darling husband passed peacefully away – my children were angelic.... Words commemorating King George v's death: "The sunset of his death tinged the whole world's sky".'

On 23 January, the coffin of the dead King was taken to Wolferton station for the journey to London. The procession

wound for two and a half miles along the muddy Norfolk roads. The new King, Edward VIII, walked bare-headed with his brothers, then Jock the white pony, led by his groom, and finally Queen Mary, her daughter and her daughters-in-law, in closed carriages. In a cage in one of the carriages rode Charlotte, King George's parrot, who had been his pet since his sailor days and who had outlived him at the last.

The King's body lay in state at Westminster Hall for four days, while 809,182 mourners filed past. On 28 January, King George was taken from London to the Chapel of the Knights of the Garter at Windsor Castle to be buried. In his funeral procession walked his four sons, five kings (of Norway, Denmark, Romania, Bulgaria and Belgium), the President of the French Republic and scores of other official mourners.

But while millions throughout the Empire saluted the passing of King George V, there were those who hoped that the new King, Edward VIII, would breathe fresh life into the monarchy. Moreover, King George had privately disapproved of many of the developments of the modern world. The twentieth century could now go on without him: hire-purchase agreements could multiply, the number of divorces could increase, popular newspapers could employ even more vulgar methods to boost their circulation, American 'talkies' could flood the cinemas, contraception could become more widespread, church attendances could dwindle.

Thankfully, posterity has not sought to judge King George merely for his personal tastes and private views. If he preferred hunting to high opera, and racy chaff to philosophic discourse, this at least brought him nearer to the common man. Although he frequently wished that he and his nation had been able to bask indefinitely under the late-Victorian sun, he was not alone in such wistful and nostalgic reveries. Despite his old-fashioned convictions, his lack of condescension was a quality rare in kings, and he gave the British monarchy an essential respectability and much-needed ballast. While it is possible to scoff that he 'never cheated, never doubted', who is to say that a battery of dynamic and unconventional views are more appropriate to kingship? Certainly, the brief reign of his successor was to prove not a watershed in the history of the British monarchy but an awkward and divisive interlude.

The King with his favourite pony Jock,
who took him on his last ride at Sandringham
and was later led in the funeral cortège.

ABOVE Edward VIII, flanked by the Duke of York and Duke of Gloucester, follows his father's coffin to Westminster Hall for the lying in state. Behind them come the Duke of Kent and Viscount Lascelles, husband of the Princess Royal.

LEFT Queen Mary in her carriage.

RIGHT The funeral procession in Piccadilly, January 1936.

Above all, the worth of a constitutional monarch is not measured by the sophistication of his intellectual pursuits but by the way in which he performs his constitutional functions. In this respect, King George stands head-and-shoulders above his predecessors. He had none of Queen Victoria's awkward partiality, and little inclination to force his views on his ministers, like Edward VII. The constitutional improprieties of his great-great-uncles George IV and William IV would have been unthinkable to him. Yet, at certain crucial times during his reign, his firm but discreet touch on the constitutional tiller helped to put events on their proper course. He had his blind spots and his prejudices, but these never came between him and his duty. In shifting times, he was the epitome of public rectitude and fair-dealing, and the British people were fortunate in the standards that he set.

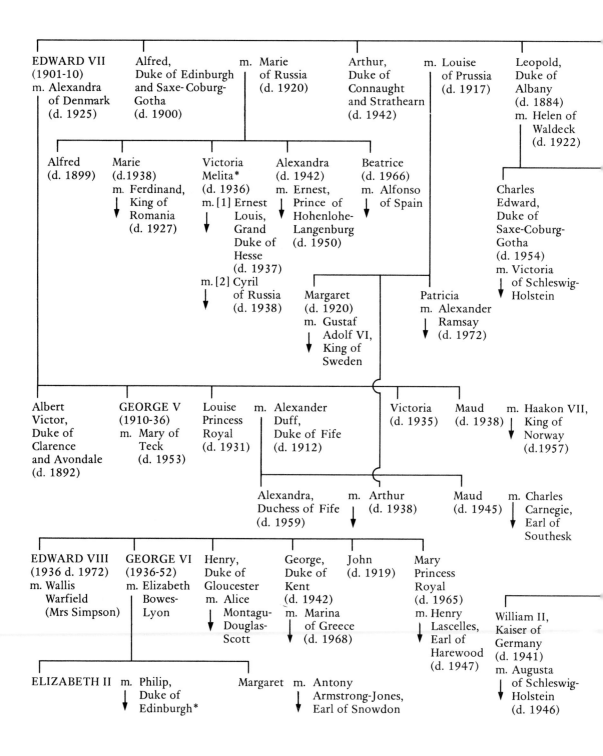

EDWARD VII
(1901-10)
m. Alexandra
of Denmark
(d. 1925)

Alfred,
Duke of Edinburgh
and Saxe-Coburg-
Gotha
(d. 1900)

m. Marie
of Russia
(d. 1920)

Arthur,
Duke of
Connaught
and Strathearn
(d. 1942)

m. Louise
of Prussia
(d. 1917)

Leopold,
Duke of
Albany
(d. 1884)
m. Helen of
Waldeck
(d. 1922)

Alfred
(d. 1899)

Marie
(d.1938)
m. Ferdinand,
King of
Romania
(d. 1927)

Victoria
Melita*
(d. 1936)
m. [1] Ernest
Louis,
Grand
Duke of
Hesse
(d. 1937)
m. [2] Cyril
of Russia
(d. 1938)

Alexandra
(d. 1942)
m. Ernest,
Prince of
Hohenlohe-
Langenburg
(d. 1950)

Beatrice
(d. 1966)
m. Alfonso
of Spain

Charles
Edward,
Duke of
Saxe-Coburg-
Gotha
(d. 1954)
m. Victoria
of Schleswig-
Holstein

Margaret
(d. 1920)
m. Gustaf
Adolf VI,
King of
Sweden

Patricia
m. Alexander
Ramsay
(d. 1972)

Albert
Victor,
Duke of
Clarence
and Avondale
(d. 1892)

GEORGE V
(1910-36)
m. Mary of
Teck
(d. 1953)

Louise
Princess
Royal
(d. 1931)

m. Alexander
Duff,
Duke of Fife
(d. 1912)

Victoria
(d. 1935)

Maud
(d. 1938)

m. Haakon VII,
King of
Norway
(d.1957)

Alexandra,
Duchess of Fife
(d. 1959)

m. Arthur
(d. 1938)

Maud
(d. 1945)

m. Charles
Carnegie,
Earl of
Southesk

EDWARD VIII
(1936 d. 1972)
m. Wallis
Warfield
(Mrs Simpson)

GEORGE VI
(1936-52)
m. Elizabeth
Bowes-
Lyon

Henry,
Duke of
Gloucester
m. Alice
Montagu-
Douglas-
Scott

George,
Duke of
Kent
(d. 1942)
m. Marina
of Greece
(d. 1968)

John
(d. 1919)

Mary
Princess
Royal
(d. 1965)
m. Henry
Lascelles,
Earl of
Harewood
(d. 1947)

William II,
Kaiser of
Germany
(d. 1941)
m. Augusta
of Schleswig-
Holstein
(d. 1946)

ELIZABETH II

m. Philip,
Duke of
Edinburgh*

Margaret

m. Antony
Armstrong-Jones,
Earl of Snowdon

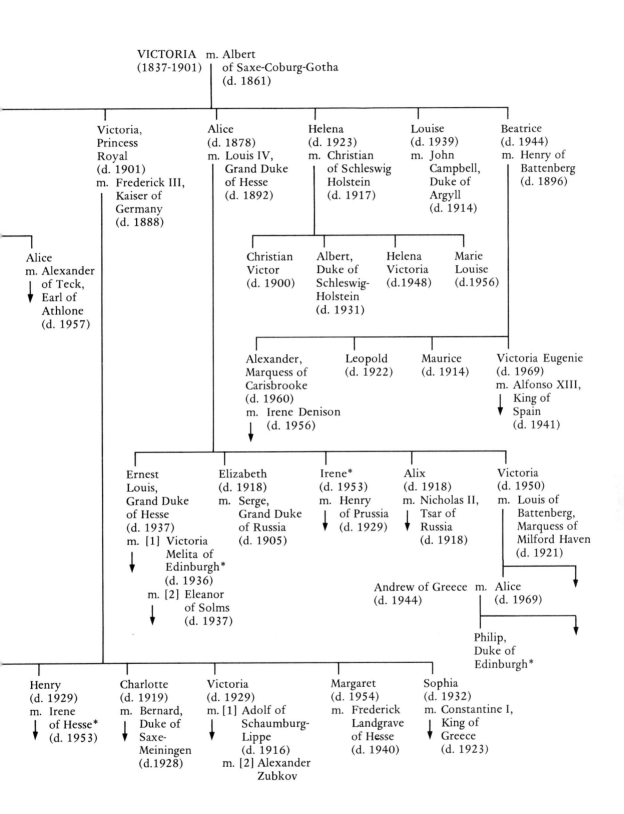

VICTORIA m. Albert
(1837-1901) | of Saxe-Coburg-Gotha
(d. 1861)

Victoria,
Princess
Royal
(d. 1901)
m. Frederick III,
Kaiser of
Germany
(d. 1888)

Alice
(d. 1878)
m. Louis IV,
Grand Duke
of Hesse
(d. 1892)

Helena
(d. 1923)
m. Christian
of Schleswig
Holstein
(d. 1917)

Louise
(d. 1939)
m. John
Campbell,
Duke of
Argyll
(d. 1914)

Beatrice
(d. 1944)
m. Henry of
Battenberg
(d. 1896)

Alice
m. Alexander
of Teck,
Earl of
Athlone
(d. 1957)

Christian
Victor
(d. 1900)

Albert,
Duke of
Schleswig-
Holstein
(d. 1931)

Helena
Victoria
(d.1948)

Marie
Louise
(d.1956)

Alexander,
Marquess of
Carisbrooke
(d. 1960)
m. Irene Denison
(d. 1956)

Leopold
(d. 1922)

Maurice
(d. 1914)

Victoria Eugenie
(d. 1969)
m. Alfonso XIII,
King of
Spain
(d. 1941)

Ernest
Louis,
Grand Duke
of Hesse
(d. 1937)
m. [1] Victoria
Melita of
Edinburgh*
(d. 1936)
m. [2] Eleanor
of Solms
(d. 1937)

Elizabeth
(d. 1918)
m. Serge,
Grand Duke
of Russia
(d. 1905)

Irene*
(d. 1953)
m. Henry
of Prussia
(d. 1929)

Alix
(d. 1918)
m. Nicholas II,
Tsar of
Russia
(d. 1918)

Victoria
(d. 1950)
m. Louis of
Battenberg,
Marquess of
Milford Haven
(d. 1921)

Andrew of Greece m. Alice
(d. 1944)   (d. 1969)

Philip,
Duke of
Edinburgh*

Henry
(d. 1929)
m. Irene
of Hesse*
(d. 1953)

Charlotte
(d. 1919)
m. Bernard,
Duke of
Saxe-
Meiningen
(d.1928)

Victoria
(d. 1929)
m. [1] Adolf of
Schaumburg-
Lippe
(d. 1916)
m. [2] Alexander
Zubkov

Margaret
(d. 1954)
m. Frederick
Landgrave
of Hesse
(d. 1940)

Sophia
(d. 1932)
m. Constantine I,
King of
Greece
(d. 1923)

Select bibliography

Ashworth, W., *An Economic History of England, 1870–1939* (1960)

Barnes, J. & Middlemas, K., *Baldwin* (1969)

Beaverbrook, Lord, *Men and Power* (1956)

Blake, Lord, *The Unknown Prime Minister: Bonar Law* (1955)

Blake, Lord, *Disraeli* (1965)

Farman, C., *The General Strike* (1972)

Fraser, P., *Joseph Chamberlain* (1966)

Gollin, A. M., *Proconsul in Politics: Milner* (1964)

Gore, J., *George V: A Personal Memoir* (1941)

Jenkins, R., *Mr Balfour's Poodle* (1954)

Jenkins, R., *Asquith* (1964)

Johnson, P., *Land fit for Heroes* (1968)

Judd, D., *Balfour and the British Empire* (1968)

Lee, Sir S., *King Edward VII* (1925–7)

Magnus, Sir P., *King Edward VII* (1964)

Makin, W. J., *Life of King George V* (1936)

Mansergh, N., *The Commonwealth Experience* (1969)

Marie Louise, Princess, *My Memories of Six Reigns* (1956)

Marsh, D. C., *The Changing Social Structure of England and Wales* (1958)

Marshall, D., *The Life and Times of Victoria* (1972)

Marwick, A., *The Deluge* (1965)

Medlicott, W., *Contemporary England, 1914–64* (1967)

Middlemas, K., *The Life and Times of Edward VII* (1972)

Montgomery, J., *The Twenties* (1957)

Mowatt, C. L., *Britain Between the Wars* (1955)

Muggeridge, M., *The Thirties* (1940)

Nicolson, Sir H., *George V: His Life and Reign* (1952)

Pelling, H., *A Short History of the Labour Party* (1961)

Ponsonby, F., *Recollections of Three Reigns* (1951)

Pope-Hennessy, J., *Queen Mary* (1959)

Read, D., *Edwardian England* (1972)

Robbins, K., *Sir Edward Grey* (1971)

Somervele, D. C., *The Reign of King George V* (1935)

Taylor, A. J. P., *The First World War: An Illustrated History* (1963)

Taylor, A. J. P. (Ed.) *Lloyd George: twelve essays* (1971)

Taylor, A. J. P., *English History, 1914–45* (1965)

Tuchman, B., *The Proud Tower* (1966)
Wheeler-Bennett, Sir J., *The Life and Reign of George VI* (1958)
Wilson, T., *Downfall of the Liberal Party* (1966)
Windsor, HRH, Duke of, *A King's Story* (1957)
Young, G. B., *Victorian England: Portrait of an Age* (2nd ed 1953)
Young, K., *Arthur James Balfour* (1963)

Index

Acts: Education Act 1902, 72;
India Councils Act 1909, 78;
Parliament Act 1911, 100,
110, 113; National Insurance
Act 1911, 106; Trade Union
Act 1913, 106; Home Rule
Act 1914, 135; Military
Service Act 1916, 136; Titles
Deprivation Act 1917, 129;
Government of Ireland Act,
1920, 161; Housing Act
1923, 1969, 177; Trade
Disputes Act 1927, 184,
192; Government of India
Act 1935, 41, 201
Albert, Prince 13–14, 21, 24, 37,
42, 51, 54
Albert Victor, Duke of
Clarence, 17, 21–2, 24–5,
27–9, 32, 36, 38, 41–4, 46, 51,
54, 185
Albert, Duke of York, 54, 98,
119, 132, 140, 165, 188
Alexandra, Queen, 13, 16–17,
21, 27–9, 32, 38, 40, 44, 46–7,
50–1, 64, 92, 97, 148, 174, 185
Alfred, Duke of Edinburgh, 37, 44
Allenby, General, 149
Amery, Leopold, 180
Asquith, Herbert, 79–80, 85, 98,
100, 109, 113, 116, 124, 129,
132, 135–6, 140, 145, 147,
159, 163, 171, 179–80
Ataturk, Kemal, 163
Australia, 28, 32, 72–4, 160, 165
Austria, 118, 132, 149, 159–60

Baldwin, Stanley, 163, 168–9,
171, 179–80, 188, 211
Balfour, Arthur James, 67–8,
72–3, 76, 78–80, 98, 113, 135,
145, 168–9, 171

Battles: Majuba Hill 1881, 31–2;
of the Marne 1914, 125; First
Ypres 1914, 125; Tannenberg
1914, 125, 148; Masurian
Lakes 1914, 125; Mons, 125,
129; Jutland 1916, 132, 140;
Somme 1916, 140, 144
Belgium, 118, 125, 144, 152, 185
Bengal, 41, 78, 103
Bevin, Ernest, 163
Bigge, Sir Arthur (Lord
Stamfordham), 68, 95, 160–1,
168, 186, 185
Birkenhead, Lord, 168, 180, 182
Boer War 1899–1902, 56, 61,
74, 158, 161
Bonar Law, Andrew, 80, 113,
135, 145, 158–9, 163, 168–9
Bondfield, Margaret, 192
Bowes-Lyon, Lady Elizabeth,
see Elizabeth, Duchess of
York
British Expeditionary Force,
124–5, 129
Bulow, Prince, 75
Burns, John, 79

Cabinet, 28, 67, 79–80, 98, 101,
109, 124, 132, 135–6, 144,
163, 174, 177, 192–3, 198,
200
Campbell-Bannerman, Sir
Henry, 79–80
Canada, 41, 72–3, 163, 165
Carson, Sir Edward, 110, 116,
135
Cetewayo, King of the Zulus,
32
Chamberlain, Austen, 113,
168–9, 171, 180
Chamberlain, Joseph, 74–5, 79,
169

Chamberlain, Neville, 169, 171,
180
Christian IX, King of Denmark,
21, 40
Churchill, Winston, 80, 110,
122, 124, 132, 168, 180, 183,
204
Clarence, Duke of, see Albert
Victor
Clynes, J. R., 174, 178
Colley, General, 32
Congress Movement, 78, 103,
192, 201
Conservatives, 41, 73, 79–80,
85, 87, 98, 100, 109, 113, 135,
145, 158–9, 162–3, 169,
178–80, 184, 188, 193,
198–200
Cook, A. J., 180, 182
Crewe, Lord, 101, 145
Curzon, Lord, 77–8, 100, 103,
145, 168, 180
Cust, Sir Charles, 186

Dalton, John, Dean of Windsor,
22, 24–5, 28, 32–3, 186
Davidson, Emily, 109
Dawson, Lord, 187, 211
De Valera, Eamon, 160–2
Disraeli, Benjamin, 28, 31
Dublin, 109, 117, 144, 162

Easter Rising 1916, 144
Edinburgh, Duke of, see Alfred
Edward VII, 13–14, 16–17,
20–2, 24, 28–9, 32, 36, 38, 40,
42, 51, 61, 64, 67, 72–5, 79,
87, 89, 92, 95, 98, 185, 217
Edward, Prince of Wales, 51,
54, 95, 97–8, 119, 131–2,
164–5, 168, 186, 188, 211–2
Elizabeth, Duchess of York, 165

Elizabeth, Princess, 187, 211
Empire, British, 33, 41, 72–3, 92, 160–1, 200–1
Entente Cordiale, 75–6
Esher, Lord, 64, 100

Fisher, Lord, 36, 129
France, 75–6, 118, 125, 131–2, 152, 177, 185, 204
Franz Ferdinand, Archduke of Austria, 92, 118
Frederick III, Emperor of Germany, 40
Frederick, Empress of Germany, 40, 46, 50
French, Sir John, 132, 139–40

Gandhi, Mahatma, 165, 192, 201
General Elections: 1906, 78–9; 1909, 85; January 1910, 85, 98; December 1910, 100; 1918, 158–9; 1922, 163; 1924, 175, 179; 1929, 188; 1931, 199–200
George v, birth, 13; childhood, 17, 20–2, 24; at sea, 24–5, 27–9, 32–3, 36–8, 41; in Germany, 40, 61; illness and death of Eddy, 42, 44; and Mary, 44, 46–8, 152, 154; and his children, 51, 54, 95, 97–8, 165; his father becomes King, 61, 68; visits Australia, 72–4; visits Germany, 74–5; visits India, 76–9, 97; his father's death, 87, 89, 92; coronation, 92, 95; and Asquith, 98, 100, 113, 117; revisits India, 100–1, 103, 106; and Home Rule, 113, 116–8, 160–2; and the War, 119, 129, 131, 136, 138–40, 144, 148, 159; and Lloyd George, 147, 158, 199; and Baldwin, 168–9, 171; and Macdonald, 174, 177–80, 193, 198, 200; and the miners' strike, 180–1, 183; his mother's death, 185; his illness, 186–8; views on

India, 201; Silver Jubilee, 205; his death, 211–12; character, 20–3, 25, 37, 44, 54, 68, 107–8, 152, 155, 164, 186, 192, 204, 212, 215
George, Duke of Kent, 54, 98
Germany, 40, 56, 61, 74–5, 89, 110, 118–9, 122, 131–2, 136, 144, 147–9, 159–60, 177, 185, 204
Gladstone, William, 13, 16, 31–2
Gloucester, Duke of, *see* Henry.
Greenwood, Sir Hamar, 160
Grey, Sir Edward, 79, 118, 122, 136, 145

Haig, Sir Douglas, 139–40, 148
Haldane, R. B., 79, 135
Hamilton, Lord George, 36
Hardy, Thomas, 100
Henderson, Arthur, 135, 145, 192, 198
Henry, Duke of Gloucester, 54, 98, 211
Hertzog, General, 185
Hitler, Adolf, 204

Imperial Conferences: 1921, 161; 1923, 169; 1926, 185; 1930, 185
Imperial War Conference 1917, 145
India, 56, 76–9, 92, 97, 100–1, 103, 106, 168, 192, 200–1, 211
Ireland, 28, 54, 82, 89, 92, 117–8, 159–62, 185
Irish Nationalists, 79, 98, 109, 117, 135
Italy, 56, 131, 185, 201

Japan, 28, 32, 76, 201, 204

Keynes, Maynard, 193
Kipling, Rudyard, 56, 110
Kitchener, Lord, 77, 92, 124, 129, 132, 139, 145
Kruger, Paul, 32

Labour, 73, 79–80, 82, 87, 98, 106, 135, 145, 159, 163, 169, 171, 174–5, 177, 179–80, 184, 187–8, 192–3, 198–200
Lansbury, George, 174, 192
Lawrence, T. E., 140
League of Nations, 122, 160, 177–8, 204
Liberals, 41, 73, 78–80, 82, 85, 87, 98, 100, 106, 113, 122, 132, 135–6, 145, 159, 163, 169, 171, 174, 178–80, 188, 193, 198–200
Lloyd George, David, 80, 85, 95, 106–7, 109, 132, 135–6, 145–8, 152, 155, 158–9, 161, 163, 168–9, 171, 188, 193, 199
London, 16, 21, 41, 92, 106, 122, 136, 152, 161, 177, 183, 192, 201, 205, 212
Louis, Prince of Battenburg, 125, 129
Louise, Princess (Princess Royal), 17, 46
Ludendorff, General, 148–9

MacDonald, Ramsay, 169, 171, 174, 177–9, 188, 192–3, 198–200
McKenna, Reginald, 109, 136, 171
Margaret, Princess, 211
Marie, Princess, 44
Mary, Queen, 42–4, 46–7, 50–1, 54, 72, 76–8, 89, 92, 95, 97–8, 100–1, 103, 106–7, 109, 119, 136, 138, 140, 152, 154, 165, 186–8, 205, 211–2
Mary, Princess (Princess Royal), 54, 98, 186
Masterman, C. F. G., 122
Maud, Princess, 17
Milner, Alfred, 145
Morel, E. D., 174
Morley, Lord, 100, 124
Morley-Minto reforms, 78, 103, 201
Mosley, Sir Oswald, 193
Mussolini, Benito, 201

Napier, Lord, 28
National Government, 193, 198–200
New Zealand, 72–3, 160, 165
Nicholas II, Tsar, 146, 148, 178

Osborne Judgment 1905, 106
Owen, Wilfrid, 144

Paget, Sir Arthur, 117
Pankhurst, Christabel, 80
Pankhurst, Emmeline, 80, 107, 109
Pankhurst, Sylvia, 80
Parliament, 79–80, 82, 85, 87, 89, 98, 100, 106, 109, 113, 118, 129, 135, 158, 162, 169, 171, 178–80, 185, 188, 198, 211
People's Budget, 85, 87, 158
Pershing, General, 148
Ponsonby, Henry, 68

Redmond, J. E., 109, 135
Roberts, Lord, 92, 110
Robertson, Sir William, 139
Royal Commission on the Coal Industry 1926, 181–2
Royal Navy, 24, 27, 41, 56, 85, 119, 124–5, 132, 136, 140, 155
Russell, Bertrand, 100

Russia, 76, 118, 125, 145, 148, 159, 162, 178
Russo-Japanese War, 76

Salisbury, Lord, 41, 54, 67, 72–3
Samuel, Sir Herbert, 193, 200
Sankey, Lord, 198
Seddon, Dick, 73
Simon, Sir John, 136
Sinclair, Sir Archibald, 200
Sinn Fein, 160–1
Smith, Herbert, 180
Smuts, Jan, 145
Snowden, Philip, 177, 198, 200
South Africa, 28–9, 32, 56, 61, 72, 92, 144, 160–1, 163, 185
Stamfordham, Lord, see Bigge, Sir Arthur
Suffragettes, 80, 82, 107, 109

Teck, Duchess of, 46–7
Teck, Duke of, 46
Teck, Princess May of, see Mary, Queen
Thomas, J. H., 107, 163, 174, 187–8, 192, 198
Trade Unions, 82, 106, 159, 162, 174, 182–3
Transvaal, the, 31–2, 56
Treaties: Brest-Litovsk 1918, 148; Anglo-Irish 1922, 162;

Locarno 1926, 184–5; London Naval 1930, 192
Trevelyan, C. P., 174, 177, 192

Ulster, 110, 113, 116, 118, 161–2
Unionists, 73, 79, 100, 110, 113, 135, 158, 162
United States, 61, 92, 147–8, 160, 165, 192

Victoria, Queen, 13–14, 16, 21–2, 24, 27–8, 32, 36, 38, 40–2, 44, 46–7, 51, 54, 61, 64, 67–8, 72, 74, 171, 205, 217
Victoria, Princess, 17, 186, 211

Wales, Princes of, see Edward VII, George V and Edward
Wales, Princess of, see Alexandra and Mary
Webb, Sidney, 174
Westminster, Statute, of, 185
Wheatley, John, 174, 177
Wigram, Sir Clive, 201
William II, Kaiser, 40, 61, 74, 129, 148–9, 159

York, Duchess of, see Elizabeth
York, Dukes of, see George V and Albert

Zinoviev letter, 179